PLANET EARTH IS AWESOME!

101 INCREDIBLE THINGS EVERY KID SHOULD KNOW

LISA REGAN

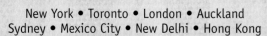
New York • Toronto • London • Auckland
Sydney • Mexico City • New Delhi • Hong Kong

This edition created in 2018 by
Arcturus Publishing Limited 26/27 Bickels Yard,
151–153 Bermondsey Street, London SE1 3HA
Copyright © Arcturus Holdings Limited

ISBN: 978-1-78828-107-2

10 9 8 7 6 5 4 3 2 1   15 16 17 18 19

Printed in China

First Scholastic edition, 2018

CH005955NT
Supplier 26, Date 1217, Print run 6379

Written by Lisa Regan
Designed by Trudi Webb

Contents

FACT 1

YOU ARE 100 KM (62 MILES) FROM OUTER SPACE!

How do astronauts know they have reached space? There is no border control out there in the Earth's atmosphere, but there is an accepted "dividing line" called the Karman line.

Blast off

The Earth is surrounded by layers of gas, or air, that get thinner as you move farther away from the planet. This is known as the atmosphere. There is no definite line where the atmosphere stops and outer space begins. However, a scientist named Theodore von Kármán (1881–1963) calculated that at around 100 km (62 miles) the atmosphere becomes too thin to allow flight in an ordinary aircraft. Anything above this height needs space launch vehicles carrying their own supply of oxygen.

SPACE

SCIENTISTS DIVIDE THE ATMOSPHERE INTO LAYERS. AS YOU CLIMB HIGHER, THE TEMPERATURE DROPS.

Life support

All the layers of the atmosphere are hugely important. Our atmosphere is what allows life on this planet. The air acts as a blanket, keeping the temperature just right for living things. It also absorbs dangerous radiation from the Sun. Oxygen molecules called ozone form a ring around the Earth (commonly called the ozone layer) that traps ultraviolet rays which would harm people, animals, and plants.

Close to Earth

The troposphere the layer close to the planet contains the oxygen that we breathe in, and the carbon dioxide we breathe out. It also contains lots of water (as a gas) and so is where nearly all our weather takes place. By contrast, the stratosphere is very dry, and jet planes often fly at this level to avoid clouds.

Exosphere — 10,000 km (6,200 miles)

Thermosphere

The Karman line — 690 km (430 miles)

Mesosphere — 85 km (52 miles)

Stratosphere — 50 km (30 miles)

Ozone layer

Troposphere — 20 km (12 miles)

Aurorae (Northern or Southern Lights) mostly occur in the thermosphere.

Higher and higher

The mesosphere begins at 50 km (30 miles) up protects our planet from falling space rocks. Most meteors and asteroids burn up in this layer before they can damage the Earth. They can be seen as shooting stars in the night sky. The next layer, the thermosphere, is where the Karman line is located, and is also where the International Space Station orbits the Earth. Finally, the exosphere is a layer of extremely thin air that fades into outer space. Satellites are commonly positioned here.

THE EARTH IS FATTER AROUND ITS MIDDLE

The Earth is usually shown as a perfect sphere, or ball shape, but that's not entirely correct. It is squashed at the top and bottom, with a bulge at the equator that makes it almost egg-shaped.

FACT 3

The Earth spins on its axis at nearly 1,600 km/h (1,000 mph).

Around and around

The great thinker and scientist Isaac Newton (1642–1727) proposed in 1687 that Earth was not perfectly round. He was right, as the diameter between the poles is roughly 42 km (26 miles) less than at the equator. It is the spinning motion that makes a spherical object bulge; it happens to other planets in our solar system, too.

High overhead

Observational satellites beam down images from above the Earth every day. The first artificial satellite was Sputnik 1, launched in 1957 to send back radio signals for research. Today there are over 1,000 satellites orbiting our planet. They transmit weather and environmental reports as well as photographs, communications, and broadcast signals.

FACT
4

You weigh slightly more at the Poles because of increased gravitational pull toward the middle of the Earth.

Changing tides

The bulge of the planet is also accentuated by the gravity of the Moon. It pulls on the oceans, making them deeper on the side facing the Moon. On the other side of the Earth, the Moon's gravity has less effect, and so the water bulges in the opposite direction. As the Earth rotates, places pass in and out of this area, causing a high tide twice a day.

All wrong!

It is impossible for a two-dimensional map to show the three-dimensional Earth properly. It is like taking the peel off an orange and trying to lay it flat in a rectangular frame. When map-makers draw the Earth's surface in 2-D, it stretches and distorts the shape and sizes of the land. Places near the equator often seem smaller than they really are. In the common Mercator projection, the continent of Africa looks a similar size to Greenland, although it is actually 14 times bigger!

The Mercator projection map is familiar but does not show the continents' real sizes.

SOME OF THE VERY EARLIEST MAPS WERE INCA MAPS MADE FROM CLAY, WHICH SHOWED 3-D MOUNTAINS AND VALLEYS.

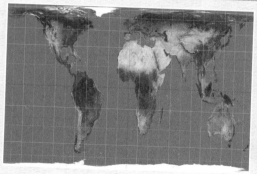

The Gall-Peters map shows the continents' size in proportion to each other.

THERE IS ONLY ONE OCEAN!

The oceans are separated by name, but are all linked together as a single, enormous body of saltwater. A unit of seawater can travel through all of the oceans in around one thousand years.

On the move

Water deep in the oceans constantly moves around the Earth in a "global conveyor belt." Wind moves the water at the surface, and temperature differences move it much deeper down. These factors create a cycle of motion. Warm water in the Atlantic Ocean is pushed north by ocean currents. As it reaches the Arctic it cools and becomes more salty, which makes it more dense, so it sinks. New surface water flows in to replace the sinking water, creating a current.

**FACT
6**

The Pacific Ocean is large enough to fit all of the world's continents in it!

That water looks familiar.

Yes, it was here 1,000 years ago...

The green sea turtle is one of many creatures that eat algae.

Life cycle

The ocean cycle helps the growth of algae and seaweed by replenishing nutrients and carbon dioxide in the cold, deep waters. All sorts of creatures, from small fish to large whales, rely on these plants as their main source of food. Tiny algae known as phytoplankton use photosynthesis to make their own food. This releases oxygen back into the water, and produces over 50 percent of the oxygen we need to stay alive.

Sea statistics

Images of the Earth from space show just how much of a "blue planet" it is. About 71 percent of the surface is covered in water. Nearly all of it is saltwater, but about 3 percent of it is fresh water in rivers, lakes, underground, or frozen in glaciers and icecaps. The largest mass of ice is the Antarctic ice sheet, holding around 90 percent of Earth's fresh water in an area nearly 14 million square km (5.4 million square miles).

FACT 7

There are up to 1 million phytoplankton in a teaspoon of seawater.

On the rise

Scientists are keeping track of the levels of the ocean because of global warming (an increase in the temperature of the Earth's atmosphere—see page 5). Rising temperatures melt ice sheets, adding to the volume of water in the ocean. It heats and therefore expands the oceans, as warm water takes up more space than cold water. Flooding is becoming more and more of a problem for towns and villages near to the coast.

EARTH DAYS ARE GETTING LONGER

The Moon has its own gravity that pulls on Earth. It is enough to slow down the speed our planet rotates, making each day last a minuscule amount longer than the one before.

In a spin

One day is the amount of time it takes for Earth to turn on its own axis. Imagine a candy lollipop on a stick. If you hold it up to the Sun and twirl the stick in your fingers, one point on the surface (representing you in your country) turns to face the Sun and then away again, making it lighter (daytime) and then darker (nighttime). The slower you twist the stick, the longer one day is.

EVERY MILLION YEARS, OUR DAYS GET 20 SECONDS LONGER. 180 MILLION YEARS FROM NOW A DAY WILL HAVE 25 HOURS!

More night? Excellent!

Endless daylight

To accurately see how the Earth turns, you should tilt the lollipop slightly forward. Then you will see that the North Pole faces the Sun the whole time, even as the Earth spins. This is how the world is positioned during summer in the northern hemisphere, meaning that for days on end, the sun doesn't set in the Arctic and it is daylight for 24 hours.

Midnight in the far north of Norway, and it is still not dark!

Days into years

A day is one full rotation of the Earth on its own axis. However, at the same time, the planet is also orbiting the Sun. A complete orbit lasts one year, or just over 365 days. Planets farther from the Sun take longer as they have more distance to travel, so one Jupiter year, for example, lasts 12 of our Earth years.

Season's greetings

The tilt of the Earth affects the seasons. Although your lollipop "North Pole" is pointing to the Sun some of the time, it is also angled away from it as it travels on some of its orbit. This gives summer and winter. Places near the equator are not affected by the seasons as the tilt does not move them away from the Sun's rays.

COUNTRIES ON THE EQUATOR HAVE TWELVE HOURS OF DAY AND TWELVE HOURS OF NIGHT, ALL YEAR ROUND.

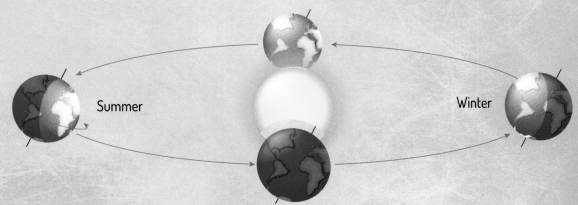

Summer

Winter

EARTH'S CORE IS AS HOT AS THE SUN

The Earth is made up of layers. The inner core is a solid metal ball with temperatures over 5,000°C (9,000°F) which is as hot as the surface of the Sun.

Recipe for a planet

Scientists cannot be exactly sure how our planet was made. It is likely that it formed out of a cloud of dust and gas pulled together by gravity. The lightest elements, hydrogen and helium, were blown away, and heavy metallic elements clumped together to form the Earth's core. Less heavy materials stayed at the surface, forming rocks and the oceans and the atmosphere.

EARTH WAS FORMED OVER 4.5 BILLION YEARS AGO.

FACT 10

The inner part of Earth's core is roughly two-thirds as big as the Moon.

It's too bright!

Deep inside

The Earth's core is made of iron and nickel, and has an inner and an outer layer. The outer layer is so hot that these metals melt and behave like a thick liquid. Although the inner core is even hotter, it is also under immense pressure, which forces the metals to stay solid. The core begins about 3,000 km (1,860 miles) beneath the Earth's surface.

Lava can be thick and gooey or runny like syrup.

Magma currents

Surrounding the Earth's core is the mantle. This is a deep layer of rock, made of silicon and magnesium. It gets hotter nearer the core, and is close to its melting point, forming magma. This gooey material moves around under the Earth's crust. Hot rocks rise toward the surface and then cool and sink again, creating currents.

FACT 11

When magma escapes onto the Earth's surface it becomes known as lava.

Land and ocean

The Earth's outer layer is the crust. The crust is thinner under the oceans, and made of heavy rock called basalt. Continental crust, which forms the land we live on, is mostly made of granite. It is lighter but thicker than oceanic crust. The crust is broken into pieces called plates, which slowly move to create continents and mountain ranges.

BASALT IS VERY DARK AND MAKES BLACK SAND.

THE POLES ARE NOT OPPOSITE EACH OTHER

The top of the world, geographically speaking, is the North Pole. It is diagonally opposite to the geographic South Pole. But there are also magnetic poles, which move around and are not opposite each other at all.

Huh??

Dividing lines

The Earth spins on its axis, an imaginary line from the bottom of the world to the top, passing directly through the core. The geographic North and South Poles, or "true poles", are the places where this line would poke out through the crust. Mapmakers use other imaginary lines, called lines of longitude, to divide the Earth into sections from north to south. These lines of longitude all meet at the true poles.

THE TRUE NORTH POLE IS NOT ON LAND, BUT ON FLOATING ICE IN THE ARCTIC OCEAN.

Polar attraction

The magnetic North Pole is more scientific than geographic. The metallic core of the Earth is moving and flowing, which creates electrical currents. This in turn generates a magnetic field. This field curves around the Earth and points straight down at the top and bottom, giving two magnetic poles. They are hundreds of miles away from the true poles!

A COMPASS NEEDLE POINTS TO THE MAGNETIC NORTH POLE, HUNDREDS OF MILES SOUTH OF THE TRUE NORTH POLE.

North and South

At the moment, the magnetic north pole is located in northern Canada. However, it is constantly on the move! Motion in the Earth's core causes changes in the magnetic field, and so magnetic north can shift from place to place. The magnetic south pole also moves around. It is not exactly opposite the magnetic north as the planet's magnetic field is not totally symmetrical.

Magnetic migration

Many creatures are thought to use the Earth's magnetic field for navigation when they migrate. Turtles swim across whole oceans to return to their birthplace when it is their turn to lay eggs. Birds tune in to the field, as well as using the Sun and the stars to find their way across continents. Dolphins and bats also sense magnetism and may use it when they travel.

Rays and sharks are sensitive to magnetic fields in the ocean.

CHALK IS MADE OF SEA CREATURES

Chalk is a very soft rock, formed millions of years ago on the ocean floor. It is made from the skeletons of microscopic plankton, crushed and compacted over time.

FACT 14

Rocks are made up of different minerals mixed together, creating a speckled effect at times.

Let's rock

The Earth's crust has many different rocks, of varying shades and hardness. They were formed in one of three ways. Chalk is a type of sedimentary rock, built up of layer upon layer of sediment (usually decayed remains of plants or animals) and subjected to heat and pressure which eventually turned them into solid rock.

Four presidents are carved into the granite at Mount Rushmore.

How cool?

Igneous rock is made from magma from inside the Earth. It cools and hardens in different ways, creating various types of rock. Granite is a very hard rock made of quartz and other minerals. It cools slowly beneath the surface, forming large crystals. Basalt has much smaller grains as it forms above the ground where it cools quickly.

Time for change

Metamorphic rocks are changed from other rocks by extreme heat or pressure. Limestone turns into marble, sandstone turns into quartzite, and mudstone turns into slate. These rocks all started as sedimentary rocks which are easily worn away by water and weather. The metamorphic process often makes them much harder and more resistant to erosion, so they are sought after as building materials.

Precious rocks

Some rocks contain crystals of minerals which can be cut and polished so they sparkle and shine. These are gemstones: precious ones such as rubies and emeralds, and semi-precious ones such as amethysts and garnets. Other rocks have their own treasures: ores are rocks containing metals such as gold, copper, and lead. They are mined and chemicals are used to separate the metal from the ore.

FACT 15

Minerals are measured on the Mohs scale of hardness. Soft talc is 1 and tough diamond is a 10.

SOME CLOUDS LOOK LIKE SPACESHIPS

That UFO your friend claims to have seen? It could simply be a lenticular cloud, like the one pictured below. These are regularly found near mountain ranges, and are a truly amazing sight.

Signs in the sky

Clouds form in the troposphere (see page 5) when humid air cools, turning the water it contains into droplets or even ice crystals. These join together until the droplets are heavy enough to fall as rain. Clouds have many different shapes depending on how fast they form and how much water they hold. White, puffy cumulus clouds are often seen when it is sunny, while towering black cumulonimbus clouds are associated with storms.

FOG IS FORMED LIKE A CLOUD JUST ABOVE GROUND LEVEL.

Heavy rains can wash away people's homes and crops.

Raining and pouring

Clouds bring rain, snow, hail, and lightning. Any water that falls to the surface of the Earth is known as precipitation. It is a vital part of the weather that helps farmers, feeds rivers and lakes where wildlife live, and of course provides the fresh water that we drink. However, too much rain can be a problem and may cause flooding in homes and across farmland.

Predicting the weather

Rain and snow, together with sunshine and wind, give our planet its weather. The weather can change from day to day in a single location, going from hot to cold and dry to wet in the blink of an eye. Experts called meteorologists study weather data to understand how they affect the planet, and forecast the weather in the future.

Weather or climate?

Long-term patterns in the temperature and other weather conditions form the climate of a place. A Mediterranean climate has hot, dry summers and mild, wet winters. Tropical climates are wet and hot, with a single season all year round. Scientists who study climate look for changes in the average, such as consistently hotter summers, or the arrival of spring weather getting earlier each year.

TERMITES ARE ADDING TO GLOBAL WARMING

The Earth's atmosphere is getting warmer because of an increase in the gases carbon dioxide and methane. What's causing this increase? Various factors, but termite emissions (yes, that means farts) are one of them!

Global warming

The gases in Earth's atmosphere act like a greenhouse, keeping the planet warm. These "greenhouse gases" include carbon dioxide (CO_2), methane, and ozone. Without them, Earth's temperature would drop well below freezing. The gases occur naturally, but their levels are rising because of extra gas made by humans and animals. More heat is trapped, making the average temperature in the atmosphere rise over the years.

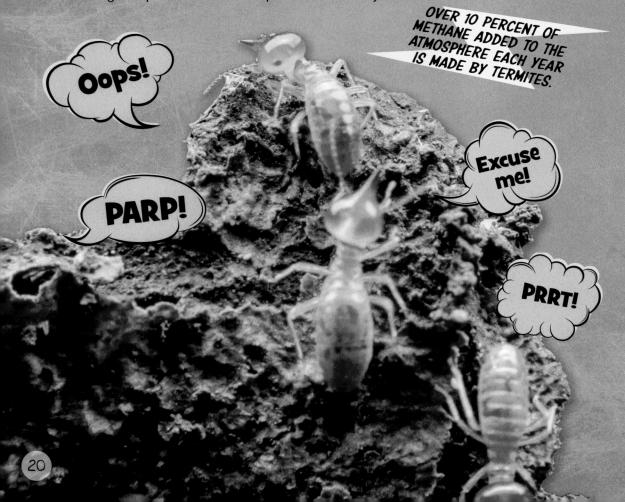

OVER 10 PERCENT OF METHANE ADDED TO THE ATMOSPHERE EACH YEAR IS MADE BY TERMITES.

What makes greenhouse gases?

Burning coal and petrol to heat our homes, power our factories, and fuel our vehicles releases huge amounts of greenhouse gases. Grass-eating animals expel methane (from both ends...) and there are now so many animals reared on farms that they contribute a large amount of gas. Cutting down trees means less CO_2 is converted into oxygen, leaving more CO_2 in the atmosphere. It all adds up to more and more gas trapping extra heat.

Aircraft use enormous amounts of fuel for each flight.

Balancing act

It is easy to upset the delicate balance of our planet. Global warming can dry up rivers and lakes, and cause droughts in areas that need more rain. Hurricanes and tornadoes can become more common as they are triggered by changes in temperature. A rise in seawater temperatures causes coral bleaching which can kill precious coral reefs.

Melting ice

Scientists are especially worried that the rise in the planet's temperature is making ice melt on mountains and in glaciers. The Arctic and Antarctic are losing much of their ice as it melts into the ocean. This extra water is adding to rising sea levels (see page 9), and leaving people and animals with fewer places to live.

FACT 18

PLASTIC BOTTLES CAN BECOME SKI JACKETS!

The modern message is that we should reuse and recycle as much as we can instead of throwing things away. Plastic causes a big problem, but recently new ways to recycle it have been found.

New from old

Some substances are more easily recycled than others. Glass can be crushed and melted and made into new bottles and jars. Paper is washed and re-rolled into new paper products. Metals are melted down and reset into all kinds of things, from car parts to food containers. Plastic, however, is tricky. There are many different types of plastic that have to be separated and reused in different ways.

AN AVERAGE OF 25 MILLION PLASTIC BOTTLES ARE THROWN AWAY EVERY HOUR IN THE U.S. ALONE.

Problem plastics

Most household waste is buried underground. Bacteria in the soil attack the waste, eating away at it. Unfortunately, plastic is a complex substance that does not break down. Recycling is tricky, and the products cannot safely be used to make new food or drinks containers. So scientists had to find other options for where to use it. They have found how to turn it into many things, from sleeping bags and toys to park benches, floor tiles, and clothing.

The squashy floors in playgrounds can be made of recycled plastic.

Waste disposal

Plastic was invented only a century ago, and is made from fossil fuels. These fuels (petrol, coal, oil, and natural gas) took millions of years to form, and we are using them faster than they can be replaced. Recycling uses fewer raw materials, and also saves energy and water during the production process. The energy saved by making a can from recycled metal would power a TV for three hours!

Help the planet

Everyone should try their hardest to save energy and stop throwing things away unnecessarily. Fix things that are broken, and give away things that you no longer want. Find new ways to use old items, and buy food with less packaging. It's really easy to use fewer plastic bottles. Buy a refillable bottle that you can use again and again.

FACT 19

A FLATFISH'S EYE SWAPS SIDES

A flatfish starts life as a "normal" shaped fish, swimming upright with an eye on each side. One eye gradually moves around to sit next to the other, so the fish can lie flat on the ocean floor. Freaky but true!

THE OCEAN IS SALTY BECAUSE OF DISSOLVED MINERALS CARRIED FROM THE LAND BY RIVERS.

FACT 20

Nearly 20 million tonnes of gold is dissolved in the ocean.

Life on the shelf

Flatfish such as the flounder are among the many creatures that live near the coast. The seabed slopes gently downward from the land in an area called the continental shelf. After a sharp drop-off, called the shelf break, the ocean becomes many times deeper. Sunlight can penetrate the coastal shallows, allowing a huge variety of life.

Sea otters live in coastal water near kelp forests.

Ocean garden

These coastal areas are known as the neritic zone. They include warm tropical waters, cooler (temperate) waters around countries such as Japan, New Zealand, Britain, and the US, and icy seas near the poles. Many things grow in the salty water, such as kelp and seagrass, which provide oxygen for fish and sharks, shellfish, urchins, and jellyfish. Numerous mammals live here as food is plentiful.

Twilight zone

Scientists divide the open ocean into layers. The top zone is called the "epipelagic zone," where sunlight can penetrate and sea plants can use photosynthesis to produce food. The epipelagic zone is deeper where the waters are clear, as sunlight can travel further down. Below that is the "mesopelagic zone" with limited light, also called the twilight zone. Even deeper is the dark "bathypelagic zone" or midnight zone.

Walking on water

Thousands of years ago, the North Atlantic was lower, and Britain was joined to the rest of Europe by the continental shelf. Fossil remains of Ice Age land creatures such as mammoths (like the tooth, pictured) have been found at the bottom of the North Sea. Similarly, Alaska (in the US) and Siberia (in Russia) were joined by a land bridge before ocean levels rose.

FACT 21

Kelp is a kind of seaweed that looks like a plant but is actually large brown algae.

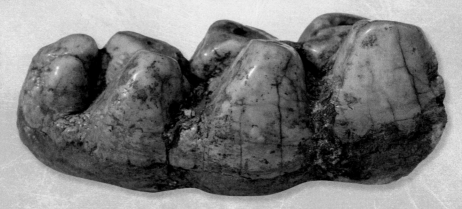

THERE ARE 3 MILLION SHIPWRECKS IN THE SEA

UNESCO estimates that around 3 million sunken ships are scattered around our ocean floors. Some are in the shallows and can be explored by divers. Others have settled in the very deepest, darkest waters.

THE DEEPEST KNOWN WRECK IS THE S.S. RIO GRANDE, OVER 5.5 KM (3.5 MILES) DOWN IN THE SOUTH ATLANTIC OCEAN.

Diving deep

Boats and ships are one of the oldest forms of travel used by people. Some of the wrecks sank thousands of years ago and can only be found using modern sonar scanning. Exploring deep waters is difficult; there is no natural light, and the pressure increases as you travel deeper and deeper; enough to crush unprotected divers and submersibles. And yet there are entire ecosystems (see page 29) living in these freezing waters..

Ocean extremes

Water presses down on people and objects much more than the air does on dry land. The pressure at 4 km (2.5 miles) deep is over 400 times that at the surface. Ocean explorers descend in small submarines called submersibles, equipped with lights, cameras, and robotic arms to collect samples. They can withstand freezing waters and immense pressure.

Underwater mountains

The ocean floor has its own watery landscape, with tall mountains and deep valleys, known as trenches. The deepest is the Mariana Trench in the Pacific Ocean. Its lowest point is the Challenger Deep, nearly 11,000 m (36,000 ft): deep enough to fit Mount Everest without it breaking the surface of the water.

Crazy creatures

The ocean is so immense that scientists have explored less than five percent of it. There are countless unknown creatures living in the ocean's depths, still waiting to be discovered. The ones we do know about have adapted to deep-water living in amazing ways. Most of them make their own light, for example, and some have giant eyes or reach enormous sizes.

THE PRESSURE IN THE DEEPEST WATERS IS THE SAME AS BALANCING A SMALL HIPPO ON YOUR OUTSTRETCHED FINGER!

A Japanese spider crab can grow to 3.7 m (12 ft).

CORAL CAN MEND HUMAN BONES

The tough outer skeleton of sea coral can be used to fix damaged bones. Doctors replace missing bone with the coral to provide support while the bone regrows.

Build it up

Corals may look like plants but they are actually animals. They are made up of tiny creatures called polyps which have a soft, delicate body. They construct a hard outer skeleton from calcium carbonate to protect themselves. Gradually, these skeletons build up to form reefs. The polyps extend their tentacles outside their protective covering to feed on tiny particles in the water, mostly at night.

FACT 24

Coral reefs cover only 1 percent of the ocean floor but are home to around 25 percent of sea creatures.

Teeming with life

There are many different types of coral, including giant star corals and smaller branching and staghorn corals. Gathered together, they provide a home for thousands of other creatures, from fish and squid to starfish and seahorses. Coral reefs form a unique ecosystem (a community of plants, animals, and bacteria living together in one habitat.) They are one of the most biodiverse habitats on the planet, comparable to rain forests (see page 34).

CORALS ARE RELATED TO ANEMONES AND JELLYFISH.

Special circumstances

A coral reef can only survive in certain conditions. Corals need clear, warm, shallow water to ensure they receive sunlight for energy. Phytoplankton (plant plankton) convert the sunlight through photosynthesis and become food for the animals living on the reef. Coral reefs are found in over 100 countries, mostly between the tropics to the north and south of the equator.

Ocean treasure

The planet's beautiful reefs are under threat. Many of the problems they face are caused by humans. Fishing, tourism, and careless divers upset the balance of a coral ecosystem and can destroy entire reefs. Excess carbon dioxide makes the ocean more acidic which can weaken coral. If the water temperature increases, the corals become stressed and turn white. This bleaching can kill them.

FACT 25

Australia's Great Barrier Reef is the largest structure made by living things on Earth.

Reefs can recover if coral bleaching is not too severe.

ABOUT A THIRD OF ALL LAND IS DESERT

Deserts aren't always hot and sandy. Some are covered in ice. They are extremely dry, with less than 250 mm (10 in) of rain in a year. Together, hot and cold deserts cover about a third of the world's landmass.

THE SAHARA DESERT IN AFRICA COVERS 12 COUNTRIES.

Super dry

Some deserts haven't seen rain for years. Hot deserts are often far from the coast, where little moisture reaches them from the ocean. Others are formed in the "rain shadow" of large mountain ranges. The damp sea air is forced to rise, making it cool rapidly and lose its moisture as rain or snow. The air becomes warm and dry beyond the mountains, creating desert conditions.

On the move

Certain tribes of people make their home in and around deserts. They live a nomadic lifestyle, and have to keep moving to survive. Their homes are usually simple shelters that can be easily packed away and reassembled. Some, like the Tuareg of the Sahara, are traders and carry goods across desert wastelands. Others, like the Bedouin of North Africa and the Middle East, herd livestock as they travel.

Nomads wear loose clothing to protect them from the Sun.

Shifting sands

The Sahara is the world's largest hot desert. It is dry and rocky, with mountains and hard, barren land. The Namib Desert in Africa is the oldest in the world, and is famous for its enormous sand dunes and dried up riverbeds. Large areas of shifting sands called ergs move around, blown by the wind, and make it hard for people to cross the land.

Survival tactics

Very few animals can survive in a desert. Some are nocturnal to avoid the heat of the daytime, hiding underground when the temperatures are at their highest. Others have adapted clever ways to stay cool, or store fat in their body for when food is hard to find. Succulent plants such as cacti and agave store water in their fleshy stems or leaves.

THE FENNEC FOX LOSES HEAT FROM BLOOD VESSELS IN ITS HUGE EARS.

SOME DESERTS ARE MADE OF SALT

The lack of rainfall in a desert can lead to some extremely unusual conditions. In some deserts, pools of surface water evaporate quickly, leaving behind huge expanses of natural salts called salt flats.

Valuable resource

Salt flats reflect sunlight and gleam a bright white. The top layer forms a crust, but may cover dangerous mud pools beneath that can suck down a person or vehicle. The biggest salt flats in the world are in Bolivia, high in the Andes Mountains. The salt there contains large amounts of lithium, an important element for producing rechargeable batteries such as those used in a laptop or phone.

BOLIVIA'S SALT FLAT WAS FORMED THOUSANDS OF YEARS AGO FROM LARGE LAKES.

Brave birds

Extreme conditions make salt lakes a difficult place for any wildlife to live. However, the Bolivian flats are the breeding ground for thousands of flamingos that turn the landscape pink every November. The birds feed on algae found in chemical-filled lakes, wading through water that would burn human skin. Temperatures drop below freezing at night, sometimes trapping the birds' legs in ice, but they simply wait until it thaws again the next day.

Harsh conditions keep the flamingos safe from predators.

Salt speeders

The largest salt lake in America is found in Utah. It is surrounded by salt flats that are up to 1.5 m (5 ft) thick in the middle. One of these, the Bonneville Salt Flats, has been the setting for several movies, and is famous for hosting motor racing and land speed records, since it is so flat, smooth, and vast.

Super salty

The Dead Sea is on the border of Jordan, Palestine, and Israel and is one of the world's saltiest seas. It is nearly ten times saltier than the ocean, which makes it dense enough to float rather than swim. It is also the lowest place on Earth as it sits 430 m (1,412 ft) below sea level.

DEAD SEA MUD CONTAINS MANY MINERALS THAT ARE SAID TO IMPROVE THE SKIN.

THE AMAZON RAIN FOREST HAS 390 BILLION TREES

Rain forests can be found in tropical and temperate areas across the globe. They receive at least 2 m (6.5 ft) of rain each year. The largest of them all is the South American Amazon rain forest.

Forest layers

Tropical rain forests are found in Central and South America, Australia, Asia, and Africa. They are notable for the large amount of rain that falls, high temperatures all year round, and the enormous trees (called emergents) that rise high above the rain forest canopy to receive as much sunlight as possible. The canopy is formed by densely packed branches that block out light from the lower layers: the understory and the floor of the forest.

FACT

29

There has been rain forest in the Amazon basin for around 55 million years.

Of all the trees, I like this one the most.

A forest feast

The world's tropical rain forests cover only about 7 percent of the Earth's surface, but about 50 percent of all living things make their home here. Lots of them are "endemic" species, found nowhere else on the planet. Many medicines in the developed world use rain forest plants as ingredients, and a lot of our foods come from the rain forest: nuts, pineapples, bananas, coffee, and chocolate, among others.

THE AMAZON RAIN FOREST IS SO HUGE IT SITS ACROSS NINE COUNTRIES.

Forest fans

Rain forests are important because of their biodiversity (the variety of plants and animals in a particular habitat) but also because of the effect they have on the planet. Their plants produce about 20 percent of the oxygen we breathe, and trap carbon in their leaves. Destroying the trees releases this carbon into the atmosphere as carbon dioxide. Trees also regulate the weather, from rainfall to global temperatures.

FACT 30

Around 50 million indigenous people live in rain forests around the globe.

Under threat

We need to protect these ancient forests, but instead, humans are exploiting them. Rain forests around the world are being chopped down at a rapid rate, to make space for crops and farming. The wood is used for building and furniture and making paper. It leaves whole communities, and thousands of animals, with nowhere to live, and can lead to floods or droughts.

FACT 31

SOME TREES ARE TALLER THAN A SKYSCRAPER

Giant redwood trees are only found naturally in California, USA, and are the tallest trees in the world. The oldest are thought to be 2,200 years old and can reach 115 m (378 ft) tall.

Green planet

Not all forests are rain forests. Trees also grow in much cooler, drier climates. The giant redwood grows near the coast and relies on thick fog from the ocean to supply it with water. Deciduous forests (see page 37) thrive across Asia and North America. They are made up of a wide variety of trees that only reach around a third the height of the redwood giants. Coniferous forests grow even farther north and consist mostly of pine, larch, and spruce trees.

RAIN FORESTS AND OTHER FORESTS TOGETHER COVER ABOUT A THIRD OF THE LAND ON THIS PLANET.

Leaves and needles

Deciduous trees change with the seasons. Their leaves turn from green to red, orange, yellow, and brown, and then fall off for the cold winters to save energy and water. Coniferous trees dominate the coldest parts of the globe. These forests are often known as the taiga. Their leaves are like needles and stay green all year, and their seeds are encased in cones.

Ground level

Cold forests have layers like the rain forest. The tall trees form a canopy that blocks out sunlight from the understory, where smaller bushes and shrubs provide a home to many woodland creatures. The forest floor is littered with dead leaves but dotted with grasses and flowers. It provides rich pickings for thousands of insects and small animals.

RUSSIA HAS LARGER AREAS OF FOREST THAN ANY OTHER COUNTRY.

Nature's grand scheme

The insects and creepy crawlies on the forest floor form part of a complex ecosystem. Beetles and ants eat fallen fruit and dead leaves, while bees, moths, and butterflies pollinate plants and help them to spread. These creatures provide food for bats and birds, which in turn are eaten by bigger predators. Very large mammals such as bears are at the top of the food web.

SAN FRANCISCO IS MEDITERRANEAN!

Certain climate types, or biomes, cover vast areas of the Earth. Others are tiny. The Mediterranean biome is named after the European sea, but also features in small areas of Chile, Australia, South Africa, and California.

Farmer's delight

The Mediterranean climate has hot, dry summers and mild winters. Hardly any rain falls in the hot months but rain and occasionally snow make the winters slightly wetter. Plants have to be able to survive the long dry periods, and the landscape is usually rocky and scrubby. However, with irrigation (supplying extra water), these areas are excellent for growing crops, and large fruit plantations, olive groves, and vineyards are a common sight.

MEDITERRANEAN CLIMATES ONLY OCCUR ON THE WESTERN SIDE OF CONTINENTS.

Popular places

Life in this climate is less harsh than in many other climate types, making them popular for habitation. California has four of the US's largest cities, and Cape Town is the second biggest city in South Africa. It is no surprise that some of the world's ancient civilizations were founded in these areas. Historical cities such as Athens, Jerusalem, and Rome have been home to people for thousands of years.

The Parthenon in Athens was built in 438 BC.

Blooming magnificent

Nature and farmers both take advantage of mild Mediterranean winters. An enormous variety of flowers bloom naturally before and after the summer drought, and brighten the whole landscape. Although small, Australia's Mediterranean region is home to over half of the whole country's flowering species. South Africa's Table Mountain has more endemic flower species than the entire UK. When the summer drought arrives, spikier plants take over, with thistles, cactus, and thorny bougainvillea flourishing.

Come and visit

Tourism plays a huge part in the economy and lifestyle of these areas. Long sunny days, blue seas, and fine foods attract tourists to the coasts and cities of European countries such as Greece, Italy, and Portugal, and Spain is the third most visited country in the world, receiving over 75 million tourists each year. This boosts employment and contributes hugely to the nations' income.

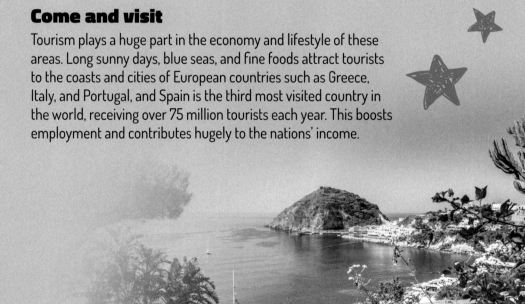

SAVANNA GRASSLANDS NEED FIRE TO SURVIVE

Savannas have only two seasons—very wet and then very dry. During the dry season, wildfires spread rapidly and burn huge areas. It may seem that plants have been destroyed, but it actually helps them flourish.

A QUARTER OF AUSTRALIA IS COVERED BY SAVANNA GRASSLANDS.

FACT 34 The drongo is a type of bird that follows wildfires, feasting on insects that are trying to escape the flames.

Burn, baby, burn

A raging wildfire can spread quickly as the wind blows and fans it across dry areas. What remains afterward, however, is an area that is cleared of dead matter. Nutrients feed back into the soil, making it more fertile. Certain plants need the flames as they have adapted so that their seeds only germinate with intense heat. Others are fire-resistant, and thrive in the space cleared by less tolerant species.

Vultures and jackals feast on animals that did not survive the drought.

A wild life

Grasslands are found in areas between deserts and forests, and cover enormous areas in Africa, Australia, South America, and India. There is too little rain in these areas for forests to survive, and so grasses dominate the vast open spaces. Animals travel great distances to find food and drink, and risk dying from thirst or starvation at the end of each dry season.

Rainy days

During the wet season, the hot, humid air rises and cools, producing heavy rains: as much as 120 cm (50 in) of rain can fall in six months. The grasses become green and the herbivores can feast again. These grasslands are home to great herds of plant-eaters, from antelopes and zebra to rhinoceros and buffalo. These, in turn, provide food for lions, leopards, cheetahs, hyenas, and jackals.

Back to their roots

Certain trees do grow in the savanna. A baobab's large trunk can store water to see it through the dry season. When it loses its leaves, it looks as if it is planted upside down with its roots in the air. The acacia tree has long roots to reach water deep underground. It is fire resistant, and can regrow from its roots if its trunk and branches are damaged. Its tiny leaves provide valuable food for giraffes.

FACT 35
The African savanna is shrinking and becoming desert at a rate of 50 km (30 miles) per year.

MANGROVE TREES GROW UNDER WATER

Forests are mostly made up of trees that grow on land and rely on fresh water. However, mangrove forests are made of around 70 species that thrive in salty water and are flooded at high tide.

Salty specialists

Mangrove forests grow on tropical coasts in mud, swamps, and sand. They have an enormous tangle of roots that are exposed when the tide goes out. These trees can cope with water 100 times saltier than most plants can handle, and survive the constant flooding and draining away of the tides. Mangroves play an important ecological role and yet are under threat from climate change and fish farming.

FLORIDA'S SOUTHWESTERN COAST IS HOME TO ONE OF THE WORLD'S LARGEST MANGROVE FORESTS.

Survival tactics

The arching roots of a mangrove tree help keep it secure in loose soil where water washes around them. They have breathing pores to take in oxygen when the water is low. These pores close tightly as the tide covers them. The plants filter out salt to obtain freshwater. Some of the salt is cast away in falling leaves or bark, while certain plants sweat it out through their leaves to form dried salt crystals.

You can actually taste the salt if you lick a mangrove leaf!

THE ROOTS OF SOME MANGROVES STICK UP LIKE A SNORKEL TO HELP THE TREES BREATHE.

A vital job

The roots of mangrove forests hold together the soil and prevent erosion of the coasts. They protect the land from storm surges and provide a safe home for small sea creatures to hide. They also absorb and store huge amounts of CO_2 from the atmosphere. A small area of mangrove trees can remove up to ten times the amount of carbon as the same sized patch of land forest.

Breeding ground

A wide variety of fish and shellfish live in mangroves, from shrimps, crabs, and lobsters to snails, oysters, and clams. Sea snakes, iguanas, and monitor lizards make their home among the roots, and larger creatures such as crocodiles and sharks lurk in the shallows. Lemon sharks give birth to their young here so they can grow and learn before they face the open ocean.

FACT 37
YOU CAN'T DRIVE AROUND GREENLAND!

The landscape and climate are harsh in Greenland, which sits inside the Arctic Circle. There are no roads to drive between towns, and people travel by boat, plane, or dog sled.

EVEN IN THE HOTTEST MONTHS, TEMPERATURES IN GREENLAND RARELY RISE ABOVE 10°C (50°F).

Tundra type

Greenland has a tundra climate type: cold and dry, with a permanently frozen layer of ground just below the surface. It receives so little rainfall that it is classed as a type of desert. Tundra covers a fifth of Earth's land area and is nearly all located around the North Pole, stretching from Canada to Russia. Very few trees can grow, and the plants are hardy and small.

Arctic animals

A surprising range of creatures live in tundra areas. They are especially well adapted to the cold and lack of food. Many of them are plant eaters, grazing on the tiny mosses and lichens that grow on the rocks and under the snow. Their coats protect them with layers of thick hairs and finer, hollow hairs to trap heat close to their body.

Life in the snow

Approximately four million people live in the Arctic, with about 40 different ethnic groups such as the Alaskan Inuit and the Saami people of Finland, Sweden, and Norway. Traditionally, they survived by hunting, fishing, and herding animals, using animal sleds to cover long distances and building snow homes and tents to live in.

Reindeer are domesticated caribou and are kept for their meat, fur, and milk.

Floating ice

Greenland is an island, but much of the Arctic is made up of sea ice rather than land. This frozen ocean water can be up to 5 m (15 ft) thick and grows or shrinks with the seasons. Polar bears trek across the sea ice to hunt for food, and whales swim in the icy waters. The sea ice is shrinking and scientists worry that the balance of nature is changing.

A POLAR BEAR CAN SMELL A SEAL LYING ON THE ICE FROM UP TO 32 KM (20 MI) AWAY!

FACT 38 EARTHQUAKES CAN MOVE CITIES!

An earthquake in Chile in 2010 was powerful enough to move the city of Concepcion 3 m (10 ft) to the west. The same year, a Californian city was moved 0.75 m (2.5 ft) south by a separate quake.

Movers and shakers

Earthquakes are at their most dangerous in built-up areas. They shake buildings and destroy roads and bridges, putting lives at risk. About a million people have died in earthquakes since the turn of the century. Walls and roofs collapse, trapping people inside, and floods and mudslides occur. Sometimes, the earth moves so dramatically that entire streets or even cities are shifted away from their original location.

THERE ARE AROUND HALF A MILLION MINOR EARTHQUAKES EACH YEAR.

Making a quake

The Earth's crust is not one solid piece. It is made up of large sections called plates that sit alongside each other. They move extremely slowly, floating on the mantle layer beneath (see page 13). When the rough edges rub together, pressure builds up. It is released as energy waves, which make the ground tremble or ripple. Ninety percent of the world's earthquakes take place around the "ring of fire" (see page 49).

Fault lines can sometimes be seen at plate boundaries.

SURPRISINGLY, TALL BUILDINGS ARE MORE STABLE IN A QUAKE THAN MEDIUM HEIGHT ONES.

Feel the force

Scientists measure the waves that cause an earthquake to determine its strength. They are known as seismic waves, and compared on the the moment magnitude scale. The waves are strongest underground, at the focus of the quake, and directly above on the surface, getting weaker as they travel farther away. A level 3 quake will hardly be felt above ground, but a level 6 quake will damage buildings.

Say what you see

The Mercalli scale is a much older way of measuring earthquakes. It describes the visible effects on the surface, both on natural landmarks and on man-made structures. It begins at I, which cannot be felt above ground, and goes up to XII, which would be total destruction of the area. It is useful for comparing damage between cities, but less so in uninhabited areas.

FACT 39 PUMICE ROCKS FLOAT ON WATER

Pumice rocks are formed when magma meets water during a volcanic eruption. The hot rocks cool especially quickly and bubbles are created inside. This makes the pumice lightweight enough to float!

Moving magma

Not all volcanoes are pointed mountains with red-hot rocks spouting out of the top—although some are. But all volcanoes have one thing in common. They are gaps in the Earth's crust where hot, molten rock can escape to the surface from deep below. This rock begins in the mantle as magma and then erupts to produce lava, gas, rocks, and ash. The gases sometimes blast the lava into the air in a spectacular, but alarming, display.

MOUNT STROMBOLI IN ITALY ERUPTS ROUGHLY EVERY HALF HOUR!

FACT 40 Most diamonds formed about three billion years ago and are brought to the surface through volcanic action.

Uprising

Volcanoes often form where two plate edges meet (see page 13). If the plates are moving together (known as a destructive boundary), one plate slides under the other and melts, producing magma which pushes up to the surface. If the plates are moving apart, it allows rock from the mantle to rise to the surface. This second type is known as a constructive boundary and usually forms shield volcanoes from very fluid lava.

Shield volcanoes have low cones and gently sloping sides.

Fast flowing

Destructive boundaries form distinctive cone-shaped, or composite, volcanoes. Their eruptions often contain a mixture of steam, dust, rock, and ash, together known as pyroclastic flow. This can travel down the slopes very quickly, destroying everything in its path.

Active or inactive?

Not all volcanoes erupt. Those that have erupted in the last 10,000 years are said to be active. Some haven't been active for longer than that, but might erupt one day, and are described as dormant. Others are not expected to erupt ever again, and are declared extinct. Dormant or extinct volcanoes often have a large sinkhole, or crater, at the top, which may fill with water to form a lake.

FACT
41

The Pacific Ocean lies on one giant tectonic plate and its edges are known as the "ring of fire", famous for volcanoes and earthquakes.

FACT 42

GEYSERS ARE USED TO GROW BANANAS!

Geysers are found in volcanic areas and are a spectacular sight. Boiling water shoots high in the air like a natural fountain. Iceland uses the hot water to grow tropical crops, such as bananas, even in polar climates.

Boiling over

A geyser is formed when cool groundwater works its way down to a hot magma chamber and is heated to boiling point. It is under such pressure that it cannot convert to steam, but explodes out through a vent in the Earth's crust. As it reaches the surface it expands into steam, blasting high into the air. Some geysers smell like rotten eggs because of the chemicals dissolved in the hot water.

YELLOWSTONE PARK IN THE US CONTAINS AROUND HALF OF THE WORLD'S GEYSERS.

Take a dip

The geothermal energy that creates geysers can also produce hot springs: pools of heated water that don't erupt but form ponds and lakes. These appear in unlikely situations, such as the freezing surroundings of Iceland. Some are too hot to touch, but others are used as natural lagoons for swimming and bathing.

In Japan, macaques use thermal pools as a spa to keep warm!

Underwater action

Some tectonic plates meet deep under the water at mid-ocean ridges. Lots of activity still takes place here. Volcanoes are pushed up and erupt underwater, or poke their tips out as volcanic islands. Deep-sea vents are formed like geysers and bubble away on the ocean floor. The minerals they contain build up into chimneys known as "smokers" and support a surprising amount of life, including giant tube worms, clams, and shrimps.

Natural resources

Living in a country that is susceptible to earthquakes and volcanic eruptions certainly has its downside, but geothermal energy also has its uses. The energy can be harnessed to drive power plants and create electricity, without using non-renewable fossil fuels or producing harmful polluting gases.

FACT 43
TSUNAMIS TRAVEL FASTER THAN A PLANE

An earthquake or volcanic eruption under the ocean can create gigantic waves called tsunami. These waves can travel over 970 km/h (600 mph) in the open ocean, which is faster than a commercial jet plane.

Wall of water

Tsunamis form far out at sea, and are only the size of a normal wave to begin with. You could safely ride over one in a boat and not even know it. However, their speed makes them deadly. By the time they reach the shore, they have gained in energy and height, forming a giant wall of water up to 40 m (130 ft) high. This crashes inland at around 30 km/h (20 mph), destroying everything in its path.

AN EARTHQUAKE HAS TO BE OVER 6.75 ON THE RICHTER SCALE TO CAUSE A TSUNAMI.

Warnings are issued if an earthquake is detected at sea.

Warning signs

Tsunamis are difficult to detect in the open ocean, but there are signs they are approaching when they near the coast. The water may pull back from the beach quite dramatically, giving people up to half an hour to get to safety. A tsunami's speed means you cannot run away from it, but should climb to high ground as fast as possible. The first wave is often followed by even bigger waves, sometimes an hour apart, so it is unsafe to go back to the shoreline until all the danger has passed.

Underwater upheaval

It isn't only earthquakes and volcanic eruptions that cause tsunamis. Japanese legends describe a giant catfish that triggers tsunamis by moving in its sleep. Of course, this isn't the case, but it is true that tsunamis are caused by a large displacement of water. For example, landslides and meteor impacts can start a tsunami.

Danger zone

Almost three quarters of tsunamis happen in the Pacific Ocean and Indian Ocean, and they are seldom seen in the Atlantic. Some have occurred in the Mediterranean Sea and along the coast of Chile. In 2004, an earthquake in the Indian Ocean caused a tsunami that killed more than 230,000 people in 14 countries, many of them in popular tourist areas.

JAPAN IS HIT BY A TSUNAMI AT LEAST ONCE A YEAR.

FACT 44 HURRICANE IRMA HAS RETIRED

So have Sandy, Katrina, and Maria. Hurricanes are given names from a list that is reused over and over. However, when a hurricane causes huge damage and loss of life, its name is removed from the list and not used again.

FACT 45 Slow-moving hurricanes produce more rain than fast-moving ones.

The naming game

Hurricanes have been given a person's name since the 1950s to help identify them. There are six lists of names that are used in rotation. However, particularly bad storms are taken off the lists; Otto was retired in 2017 and replaced with Owen. Tropical storms are only called hurricanes when they form over the Atlantic Ocean. Pacific storms are called typhoons and ones in the Indian Ocean are called cyclones. Each of these has a separate set of girls' or boys' names to choose from.

Cooking up a storm

Hurricanes form in the tropics where the ocean temperature is above 27°C (80°F). The warm water heats up the air so it rises and cools, creating huge clouds. This leaves an area of low pressure underneath. Air rushes in to take its place, forming a cycle that spins and grows. As it rotates ever faster, it creates a circular area in the middle called the "eye" which is typically about 20–50 km (12–30 miles) wide.

The eye of the storm is calmer than its surroundings.

Devastating damage

Tropical cyclones usually slow down and become weaker when they reach land as they no longer receive energy from the warm ocean. They continue their journey inland for many miles, though, causing torrential rainfall and high winds. Huge waves known as storm surges destroy coastal towns. People are left without homes or possessions, and many lives may be lost.

FACT
46

In the southern hemisphere, cyclones swirl clockwise. In the northern hemisphere, they move in the opposite direction.

Storm protection

A hurricane is classified on the Saffir-Simpson scale, where a category one causes the least damage. The scale goes up to five, classed as catastrophic, with wind speeds of over 250 km/h (155 mph) and storm surges over 5.5 m (18 ft) high. Buildings in danger zones are often made with reinforced concrete and shatterproof glass to protect them from debris being blown at high speeds.

DOME-SHAPED BUILDINGS ARE ABLE TO WITHSTAND HURRICANES BETTER THAN MOST OTHER BUILDINGS.

TORNADOES SOMETIMES TRAVEL IN PACKS

A tornado is a high-speed wind that forms at the base of a stormcloud and spirals across the land. It may have a single funnel or more than one, sucking up anything in its path.

Hey, sucker!

Tornadoes are also called twisters or whirlwinds. They are formed when warm air containing lots of moisture rises and meets colder air at the bottom of a thundercloud. The Earth's rotation causes this updraft to revolve (like water curling down a drain). The funnel of twirling wind can spin at speeds over 480 km/h (300 mph) and travel at 110 km/h (70 mph), gathering dust and other objects as it passes.

FACT 48
Tornadoes can happen at any time but are most common between 3pm and 9pm.

A MAN IN MISSOURI WAS CARRIED 389 M (0.25 MILE) BY A TORNADO!

Let's twist again

The US and Canada get more tornadoes than any other countries: an average of 1,000 each year in the US alone. The UK has around 60 per year, which is more for its size than any other nation! The south-central US is nicknamed "Tornado Alley" since it receives an especially high frequency, usually in the early spring.

Storm chasers

Scientists find it hard to predict when and where a twister will occur. Not all storms produce one, and a typical tornado lasts for only a few minutes, making them difficult to study. Some fanatics chase storms for a hobby or to record the conditions. Most people prefer to wait until the twister has passed, and the safest place is below ground in a cellar or basement.

Even large trucks can be wrecked in the path of a tornado.

Pick me up

Whirlwinds sometimes swirl across deserts or lakes, whisking up sand and dust or water as they pass. These are known as dust devils or waterspouts. A waterspout may pick up small creatures along with the water, later depositing fish and frogs a fair distance away! Not all dust devils are connected to stormclouds, but they work in a similar fashion, as a rotating column of wind that moves across the landscape.

FACT
49

A funnel cloud is only classified as a tornado if it touches the ground.

BLUE ICE IS STRONGER THAN WHITE ICE

Recently formed ice is full of air bubbles and reflects white light. Older ice has been under extreme pressure. As the air is squeezed out, the ice reflects less white light, and looks blue. It's strong enough to land a plane on!

Ocean disasters

Icebergs form when the end of a glacier breaks free and floats into the ocean. They look like mountains drifting in the water. The largest are over 75 m (240 ft) high and can be over 600 m (200 ft) long. Smaller pieces of ice are known as growlers, about the size of a car, and bergy bits, the size of a house. Small icebergs can be especially dangerous to ships as they sit low in the water and are hard to see or track.

AN ICEBERG MAY FLIP OVER, CAUSING TSUNAMIS.

On the move

Glaciers are rivers of ice that grind their way down a valley. They grow bigger as snow falls on top of them. Glaciers move very slowly compared to a normal river, creeping forward on a layer of melted water underneath. Most glaciers move around 1 m (3 ft) per day but some travel faster than that. When the front part (called the snout) reaches the ocean or a lake, it breaks off as an iceberg.

An iceberg breaks free in a process known as calving.

FAST-MOVING GLACIERS PRODUCE BIGGER ICEBERGS THAN SLOW-MOVING GLACIERS.

Ice from the ocean

Sea ice is not formed on land, but is frozen seawater. The pieces are flatter than icebergs as they expand out rather than up. They can float on the surface in small circles, called pancake ice, or vast floes which are over 20 m (65 ft) across. About 15 percent of the world's oceans are covered by sea ice during the coldest months.

Mountain disaster

Icebergs do not usually pose a danger to people, but snow and ice on mountains can be deadly. An avalanche is a gigantic mass of snow and ice falling down a mountainside. It may be triggered by skiers or hikers crossing unstable areas, or when heavy snowfall adds too much weight to the existing snow. The snow can tumble down at up to 130 km/h (80 mph) destroying everything in its path and killing or trapping anyone in its way.

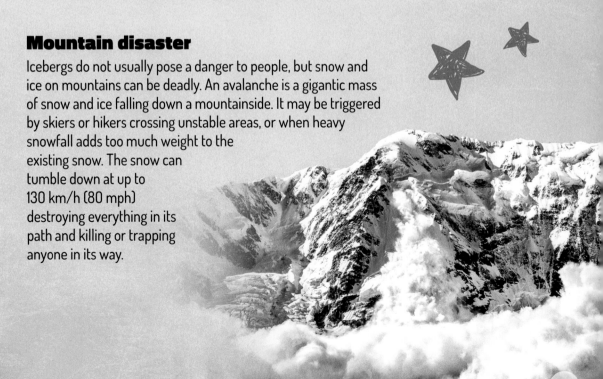

THE ARAL SEA IS DISAPPEARING

The Aral Sea is in Central Asia, and in the 1960s it was the fourth largest lake in the world. Since then, it has shrunk to just 10 percent of its original size and the surrounding land has turned to desert.

From water to dust

The Aral Sea used to be a giant saltwater lake, full of fish and fishing boats. People relied on it for food and jobs, catching fish and using the land around it to grow crops. In the 1960s the Russian government diverted the rivers that flowed into the lake to use the water on farms. The Aral Sea began to dry up, leaving a landscape of salty sand, dry soil, and stranded ships.

THE ARAL SEA USED TO SUPPLY AROUND ONE SIXTH OF ALL THE FISH EATEN IN RUSSIA.

Naturally dry

An area that has too little water is said to be suffering from a drought. This may happen naturally, in climates that receive very little rainfall. The Atacama Desert in South America is one of the driest places in the world, with some places receiving no rainfall from one year to the next. Lake Eyre in Australia fills with water during the monsoon season, becoming the country's largest salt lake, but evaporates in the dry season to become a giant salt flat (see page 32).

NASA tests space equipment in the Moon-like Atacama desert!

Manmade disasters

Droughts are often caused by human activity. As well as diverting rivers for irrigation, people build dams to provide electricity, reducing the volume of water that reaches land downriver. Clearing trees also damages the land's ability to retain water, creating new areas of desert. Severe droughts bring famine and disease as crops fail and sanitation becomes poor.

Overspill

The opposite of drought is flooding, and it can also be a disaster. Heavy rains or melting snow cause rivers to break their banks and spill water over the land around. Many countries in South-East Asia have two seasons: the dry season and the wet season, when torrential downpours called monsoon rains flood the area. Some villages are built on stilts to keep them safe from rising water.

METEORITES HIT EARTH EVERY DAY

Chunks of rock constantly zoom around in space. Some of them head toward our planet, and those that make it through the atmosphere and land on Earth are called meteorites.

Space rocks

Thousands of rocks orbit the Sun in an area between Mars and Jupiter known as the asteroid belt. They are leftovers from when the planets were formed. Sometimes their paths cross Earth's orbit, or two asteroids crash together and broken pieces are sent spinning into Earth's path. Many of them burn up as they enter the Earth's atmosphere but some slam into the ground, leaving a circular crater. They can leave debris called meteorites, which can be pebble-sized or weigh up to 100 kg (220 lbs).

ROCKS THAT BURN UP CAN BE SEEN AS METEORS OR SHOOTING STARS IN THE NIGHT SKY.

Keeping watch

A large asteroid or meteorite hitting Earth could cause a huge disaster. A rock measuring around 20 m (65 ft) broke through the atmosphere above Russia in 2013 and created a shock wave that injured 1,200 people. Larger rocks could wipe out buildings and roads and possibly cause a tsunami. NASA tracks large objects in space to check which will pass close to the Earth, giving warning of any possible danger.

Wipeout

Asteroids have hit the Earth at various times in its history. The impact releases enormous amounts of energy, causing fires and throwing rocks and dust into the air. Scientists believe that an asteroid impact wiped out the dinosaurs, 65 million years ago, by filling the sky with dust and blocking out the Sun. The climate cooled dramatically and plants and creatures could not survive.

YOU SHOULDN'T SHOWER IN A LIGHTNING STORM

Lightning is a flash of electrical energy that passes between clouds and the ground. This electricity can strike the water pipes in a house and electrify the bathroom. Yikes!

Fatal attraction

Lightning occurs in storm clouds when frozen raindrops bump into each other and create an electrical charge. These charges pass between the base of a cloud and the ground, heating the surrounding air to an extremely high temperature (over 20,000°C or 36,000°F). Lightning is attracted to metal, including pipes in your bathroom and kitchen. Water also helps conduct electricity, so it isn't safe to sit in the tub or do the dishes, either!

THE SOUND WAVES FROM THUNDER CAN BE STRONG ENOUGH TO CRACK WINDOWS.

Deadly strike

Lightning is lazy, and will use anything taller than its surroundings as a target to reach the ground quickly. That could be a tower, a mountain, a lone tree, or you, if you don't take cover. Beware, also, as lightning can strike up to 16 km (10 miles) away from the middle of a storm. More people are killed or injured in America each year by lightning than by tornadoes or hurricanes.

Bright sparks

Lightning doesn't always travel down to the ground. If you watch a slowed-down video, you will see that it sometimes journeys upward, from ground to cloud. It can move sideways, from one cloud to another, and even flash around within a single cloud. Almost three quarters of lightning stays within the cloud where it was formed, creating "sheet lightning" that glows across the sky.

Sounds scary

A spark of lightning causes a shock wave and makes the air around it vibrate, producing the familiar sound of thunder. Sound travels nearly a million times slower than light, which is why you will see the flash before you hear the crash. If you are close to the storm, the thunder will sound like a whip crack, becoming a longer, lower rumble as the storm moves away.

Our planet has around 45,000 thunderstorms every day.

FACT 54 ROCKS CAN BE FOLDED

The world's biggest mountain ranges are made of rocks that have been crushed and folded. The Himalayas, Alps, and Andes are all fold mountains. Smaller rocks can also be folded under pressure, creating spectacular visual effects.

Around the world

Fold mountains are the most common type of mountain. They are found all over the world: the Rockies and Appalachians in the US, the Urals between Europe and Asia, Australia's Great Dividing Range, and the Atlas mountains in Africa are other examples. Some were formed over 200 million years ago, while others are relatively young ranges, only 10 to 25 million years old. These younger mountains tend to be more rugged with high peaks, as they have not been subjected to so many millennia of erosion.

FACT 55

New Zealand's Southern Alps are young mountains and did not exist until 5 million years ago.

Making a mountain

Most fold mountains are found on the edge of a plate boundary. The rock layers are pushed upward as two convergent plates crash into each other. The rocks at the edge of a plate are often weaker than those in the interior, making it easier for them to be squeezed and folded over one another. It is much the same as a car crash: two vehicles colliding with each other will crumple and bend.

FACT 56

Mountain ranges can link together to form a long chain known as a cordillera.

Steep and high

Mountains can also form at faults or cracks in the Earth's crust. Some sections of the crust collapse inward and down, while others are pushed up in enormous blocks that form sheer, steep rock faces. The Sierra Nevada range in the US is a spectacular example of steep cliff-like mountains. It contains Mount Whitney, the highest peak in the contiguous US.

Up and down

Mountains are constantly changing landforms. Erosion wears away the rocks and gravity carries the particles down the slopes. A huge landslide in 1991 caused Mount Cook in New Zealand to shrink by 10 m (33 ft). However, many mountains are growing slightly bigger, as the forces pushing them together continue to act on them. The Himalayas are already huge, and are growing by around 20 mm (0.75 in) each year.

THE MATTERHORN IS A FOLD MOUNTAIN THAT HAS BEEN ERODED BY GLACIERS.

FACT 57 EVEREST IS NOT OUR TALLEST MOUNTAIN

The Himalayan mountains contain ten of the world's 14 highest peaks, including Everest. But some of the world's tallest mountains would dwarf those peaks if the ocean wasn't covering them.

ANYTHING OVER 610 M (2,000 FT) IS CLASSIFIED AS A MOUNTAIN.

Tallest or highest?

A mountain can be measured from sea level to its peak. In that way, Everest is the highest, at 8,850 m (29,000 ft). However, mountains such as Mauna Kea, in Hawaii, are partially hidden underwater. Measured from its base to its peak, Mauna Kea is 10,203 m (33,374 ft), making it taller but not actually higher. Its height above sea level is only 4,205 m (13,796 ft)—less than half the height it would need to be the world's highest.

Looks pretty tall to me!

Bubbling under

The longest mountain range on Earth is mostly hidden under the ocean. It stretches from the Arctic Ocean down to the south Atlantic for over 16,000 km (10,000 miles) and consists of strings of volcanoes. Underwater volcanoes are formed in the same way as they are on land, by the Earth's plates moving and allowing hot rocks to rise up through a gap. Around 90 percent of the mid-Atlantic ridge is hidden under water.

The peaks of volcanoes poke out of the water as islands.

THE HIGHEST MOUNTAIN IN THE SOLAR SYSTEM IS OLYMPUS MONS ON MARS, OVER TWICE THE HEIGHT OF EVEREST.

Reach for the Moon

There is a third mountain on Earth that can stake a claim to the title of tallest: Mount Chimborazo in Ecuador. It is not the highest above sea level, but because of the bulge of our planet around the equator (see page 6), Chimborazo's summit is the farthest point from the middle of the Earth. It is also the point on Earth's surface that is the closest to the Moon!

Head for heights

There are 14 mountains that reach over 8,000 m (26,247 ft) above sea level, and they form an elite list for mountaineers wishing to climb them. All of them are in Asia. The "eight-thousanders" all have summits in the death zone, where there is too little oxygen to breathe without help.

MOUNTAIN CLIMBING IS BANNED IN BHUTAN

Bhutan is a small country in the Himalayas and contains several high peaks, but no mountaineering has been allowed there since 2003. Hikers are prevented from going above around 4,000 m (13,000 ft).

OVER 4,000 PEOPLE HAVE CLIMBED EVEREST, BUT MORE THAN 290 PEOPLE HAVE DIED TRYING.

No-go zone

Many of Bhutan's peaks are considered sacred, and the Bhutanese government prohibited the climbing of them out of respect. Additionally, there are no rescue teams to help people in the case of an emergency. Mountain climbing is a dangerous activity, and peaks in most countries have search-and-rescue teams close by if climbing parties get stuck. In 1996, eight people died in one day attempting to climb Everest; as a consequence, safety measures were drastically improved.

Seven summits

The first person to climb the highest mountain on each of the seven continents was the American, Richard Bass, in 1985. Everest is, of course, the highest and ticks Asia off the list. Australia's Mount Kosciuszko is the smallest of the seven. The easiest to climb is Africa's Mount Kilimanjaro, and its summit can be reached just by hiking.

The high life

Life in the mountains can be tough. Mountaineers often carry their own oxygen as it becomes harder to breathe at altitude. Around 2 percent of the world's population live permanently in these conditions. Scientists have found that the bodies of people living in the Andes, the Himalayas, and Ethiopia have adapted to cope better with breathing this "thin" air.

South African Bernard Goosen climbed Kilimanjaro in a wheelchair—twice!

KILIMANJARO HAS GLACIERS ON TOP EVEN THOUGH IT IS NEAR THE EQUATOR.

On top of the world

Many animals have also adapted to live in low-oxygen environments. There is as little as 40 percent of the oxygen high in the mountains, and animals such as llamas have more red blood cells, allowing their blood to react better with the limited oxygen. Llamas and mountain goats have feet that give them the best possible grip on uneven, rocky ground.

YOU DRINK THE SAME WATER DINOSAURS DRANK!

The Earth has a limited amount of water that is constantly recycled. It is the same water that the dinosaurs drank, and it will still be here millions of years into the future.

RAINDROPS ARE SPHERICAL AT FIRST AND THEN TAKE THE SHAPE OF A JELLY BEAN.

Around and around

This constant flow of water is known as the water cycle. Water enters the atmosphere in its gaseous form, and condenses as it cools, forming raindrops. These fall to Earth and the water collects in puddles, rivers, lakes, and the ocean. It evaporates again, entering the atmosphere, and the process repeats itself endlessly. Of course, the water can be diverted, and used for drinking, sanitation, irrigation, or manufacturing, but ultimately it keeps its place in the water cycle.

Into the air

Liquid water gets into the air by evaporation and also by transpiration. With evaporation, heat energy turns the water from a liquid into a gas and it rises upward before cooling again to form clouds. Transpiration takes place when plants pull water up from the ground and release it through their leaves. A single corn plant loses nearly 2 l (0.5 gallon) of water per day, which is over 200 l (52 gallons) in one growing season.

A RAINDROP CAN SPEND TEN DAYS IN THE SKY BEFORE IT FALLS.

Rain or shine?

There is water in the air even on a cloudless day. It sits in tiny droplets that are too small to see. Once these combine with tiny particles of dust or smoke, they gather and grow into clouds. There are ten basic cloud types, varying from high, wispy cirrus clouds made of ice crystals to giant, anvil-shaped cumulonimbus clouds that bring very heavy rain.

Acid rain

Clearly, the type of water that evaporates will affect the rain that eventually falls. Unpolluted rainwater is slightly acidic, with a pH of about 5.6. The rain that falls in parts of Costa Rica has a pH of 2 or lower, which is extremely strong acid. It has evaporated from the Laguna Caliente, a volcanic lake which sometimes even blasts out its acidic water as a geyser.

Laguna Caliente is on top of the still-active Poás Volcano.

FACT 60
THE HUDSON RIVER FLOWS IN TWO DIRECTIONS

Its Native American name means "river that flows two ways." It begins by flowing south near its source (the Adirondack Mountains in New York state) and then, near the Atlantic, it swaps and flows north with the tide.

Back and forth

Most rivers work their way downhill until they reach the coast at the river mouth. Some rivers flow into a lake or another river. Rivers that have their mouth at the ocean may be affected by the tides, with water flowing back upriver at high tide. The Hudson River in New York is unusual as it has an extremely long (246 km/153 miles) estuary (see page 75), so nearly half of its length is affected by tides.

Are you coming or going?

THE SEVEN SPIKES ON THE STATUE OF LIBERTY'S CROWN REPRESENT THE SEVEN CONTINENTS.

Meeting the ocean

An estuary is an area where a freshwater river meets the saltwater of the ocean. It can create a unique ecosystem, inhabited by creatures and plants that can survive in brackish (partly salty) water. Some rivers form wide deltas as they slow down in their lower stages and deposit any sediments that have been carried along. The soil in a delta is usually very fertile.

Starting point

The beginning of a river is called its source. It may start as a small mountain stream or spring, a melting glacier, or an outlet from a lake. Other streams and rivers, called tributaries, might join along the way. The world's longest river, the Nile, has two main tributaries that flow from lakes in different countries. It finally meets the Mediterranean Sea after flowing for 6,670 km (4,145 miles) through ten countries.

Who lives here

Rivers provide a home for a huge variety of freshwater wildlife, including fish, birds, amphibians, and mammals. Bull sharks are notorious for leaving the ocean and swimming far upriver. River dolphins used to live in some of the world's largest rivers but are struggling to survive among heavy boat traffic and in polluted water.

FACT
61

The Nile is long enough to flow across the US, from New York City to LA, and halfway back again!

Pink dolphins live in the Amazon and, unlike sea dolphins, have a flexible neck.

WE DON'T KNOW THE DEPTH OF THE CONGO

But we do know that it's the deepest river in the world. Scientists have tried to measure it using equipment meant for the ocean, and think it is over 220 m (720 ft) deep. That's deeper than much of the Irish Sea!

Split personality

The Congo River is only the ninth-longest in the world, but in its lower reaches it is deep and fast. The river runs across central Africa, crossing the equator along the way. To begin with, it is a slow and winding river, but for the last 320 km (200 miles) it flows furiously with whirlpools and rapids. Its unique character makes it home to a huge number of endemic species (ones found nowhere else in the world).

Are you sure it won't be higher than my chest?

Upper river

The Congo is unusual as the upper section of a river, its "youthful" stage, is usually the steepest and fastest part, with lots of erosion. Water swirls around obstacles such as stones or rocks on the riverbed. It picks them up and they roll and bump along, cutting steep, narrow valleys as they go.

Middle river

As a river slows it reaches its "mature" stage, winding across gentler landscapes. The course may bend dramatically in a series of S-shaped curves called meanders. The river erodes the outside edge of a bend and leaves deposits on the inside edge, re-routing the water until it eventually cuts off the corner, leaving an oxbow lake.

Lower river

Two rivers, or tributaries (see page 75) join at a point called the confluence. You can sometimes see this happening, such as when the Amazon and Negro Rivers meet (pictured below). Eventually, most rivers will reach their "old age", moving across flatter land and flowing slowly to the sea. A river always flows slightly downhill, even if it looks flat.

THE RIO NEGRO FLOWS ALONGSIDE THE RIVER AMAZON FOR 6 KM (3.7 MILES) WITHOUT THE DARK AND PALE WATERS MIXING.

Erosion on the curves of a river can change its course.

NIAGARA FALLS IS MOVING BACKWARD

There are three waterfalls at Niagara, on the US/Canadian border. So much water flows over their edges that the rock beneath is being worn away, and the falls are moving back up the river every year.

Breaking down

A waterfall forms where a river flows off a rocky ledge. When the falls occur over layers of rock with different hardnesses, the force of the water wears away both rocks, but the soft rock erodes much faster. It creates a plunge pool beneath, and the swirling action of the water breaks away more soft rock, creating an overhang. This may eventually break away, moving the waterfall back up the river.

NIAGARA FALLS ARE THE WIDEST AND MOST POWERFUL FALLS IN NORTH AMERICA.

FACT 64

Enough electricity is made by the Niagara Falls power plants to power 3.8 million homes.

Moving fast

The Niagara River splits three ways at the falls, to flow around two small islands. It forms the Horseshoe Falls, named for its curving shape, the American Falls (on the US side of the border) and the Bridal Veil Falls, the smallest of the three. The Horseshoe Falls used to erode so quickly that it moved backward over 1 m (3 ft) every year, but the flow of the river has been reduced so it now erodes around 0.3 m (1 ft) every 10 years.

Use the power

Niagara Falls is an example of a block waterfall, where masses of water descends from a wide stream. The huge volumes of water are what make Niagara such an amazing sight. Some of the water can be diverted from the river above the falls to generate electricity in hydroelectric power stations. A series of gates are raised and lowered to channel the water to the stations, or allow it to flow directly over the falls.

Angel Falls is named after an aviator who crashed his plane at the top.

Amazing falls

The world's highest waterfall is the Angel Falls in the jungle of Venezuela. It is more than 15 times the height of Niagara, tumbling off the edge of a flat-topped mountain called a tepui. The water falls so far that in the warm, dry season when the river's flow is reduced, the water evaporates before it touches the ground and forms a mist.

GLACIERS CAN BE EXPORTED!

The ice contained in glaciers can be tens of thousands of years old, and free of modern-day pollution. That makes it appealing to use as ice cubes in drinks, for drinking water, and for cutting large blocks to make beautiful sculptures.

Luxury ice

The governments of glacial areas such as Alaska and Greenland authorize the harvesting of ice from ancient glaciers. To reduce environmental impact, the ice is taken from sections that have already calved off the glacier (see page 59). Large ice blocks are transported to be used in ice sculpting competitions around the world, and millions of ice cubes are sold to luxury hotels for their clarity, purity, and the fascinating crackle and pop they make as they melt!

Let it snow

A glacier is a river of ice, but it is not the same as a frozen river. Some free-flowing rivers may freeze over in winter, but a glacier is made entirely of snow that has fallen and frozen year after year. If the snow doesn't melt, it becomes compacted into an ice sheet. Most glaciers are found in mountain ranges, creeping slowly down and carving U-shaped valleys as they move.

Fitz Roy glacier is in the Patagonian mountains in South America.

Ice cycle

Lots of glaciers have been around since the last Ice Age, which ended around 11,500 years ago. During that time, polar ice extended from the North Pole to as far south as Great Britain and Ireland, Germany and Poland, and the Midwestern US. An Ice Age, or glacial period, lasts for thousands of years, and is followed by a warmer period called an interglacial.

FACT 66

There have been eight Ice Ages in the last 750,000 years.

Disappearing act

Glaciers are found around the world, from Peru and New Zealand to Canada and Russia. They even occur in hot countries such as Tanzania and Indonesia, high in the mountains. However, many glaciers are getting smaller, or retreating, as global temperatures rise. Scientists are concerned that the retreat rate is getting faster, and some of our most stunning glaciers might disappear in the next 20 years. Retreating glaciers affect mountain ecosystems, home to animals like the snow leopard.

SOME LAKES CAN EXPLODE!

Lake Nyos in Cameroon is one of a handful of lakes that contains so much carbon dioxide, it can explode. It has already destroyed homes and taken lives, and is still a potential danger.

LAKE BAIKAL IN RUSSIA CONTAINS MORE WATER THAN ALL OF THE US GREAT LAKES PUT TOGETHER.

Dangerous waters

The bottom of Lake Nyos (pictured below) hides a layer of carbon dioxide which leaks into the water. When this is disturbed, it bubbles up and erupts. The explosion is not the only danger. The CO_2 which is released will suffocate local people unless they can get to higher ground. The boundaries of the lake are under permanent threat of breaking, which would cause flooding and a large-scale release of more CO_2.

Beavers build dams that create ponds and lakes.

Glacier lakes

The movement of a glacier can form a lake. As the ice pushes down a mountainside it scrapes away a U-shaped basin and forces rocks and stones in front of it. If the glacier retreats or melts, these rocks form a natural barrier to hold water in long, narrow lakes. The Great Lakes in the US and Canada are the largest examples in the world, and the Lake District (UK), lochs of Scotland, and fjord lakes of Norway are all stunning glacial creations.

Crater lakes

Lakes are a common occurrence on the tops of volcanic peaks. Lake Nyos is one example. A volcanic eruption leaves a crater which forms a natural basin for a lake to form. Sometimes the whole magma chamber collapses, leaving a bigger crater called a caldera. These fill with rainwater or melted snow and ice to give crystal clear lakes.

Make a lake!

There are millions of lakes on this planet. They are bodies of water surrounded by land, and are formed in various ways. Some are tiny and are known as ponds. Others are big enough to be called seas, such as the Caspian Sea, which is the largest in the world (although not the deepest, that is Lake Baikal). Both the Caspian Sea and Lake Baikal were formed by movements in the Earth's crust, creating a natural dip in the rocks.

LAKE BOHINJ IN SLOVENIA IS A GLACIAL LAKE DAMMED BY ROCKS.

PREDJAMA CASTLE IS BUILT IN A CAVE

Caves can be found on the coast or in rock formations inland. The spectacular Predjama Castle in Slovenia is built partway up a cliff, in the mouth of a cavern, to help defend it from invaders.

GYPSUM IS A ROCK SO SOLUBLE THAT A TRUCK-SIZED BLOCK WOULD DISSOLVE IN 18 MONTHS IF PLACED IN A RIVER.

Going underground

Predjama Castle is located at the entrance to a whole network of caves and tunnels. It is typical of a karst landscape—an area of soft rocks that can be dissolved and eroded by water. Karst countryside has steep cliffs and underground passages and caverns, often with rivers running through them. You may also find sinkholes: large chasms where the surface rock has collapsed into the empty space beneath.

Dripping water contains dissolved limestone from the rocks.

Rock formations

Cave systems have their own unique interior design features. The best known are stalactites and stalagmites. Both are formed by the constant dripping of water from the cave roof. Minerals that have dissolved in the water collect to form solid trails hanging from the ceiling (stalactites), much like an icicle hanging down. Stalagmites grow upward from the floor as the minerals collect where the water drips.

Taking shelter

Caves provide natural shelter from the cold and rain. Cavemen weren't entirely stupid, you know! However, prehistoric cave dwellers had to share their space with bears and other wild animals, and were more likely to make their own shelters elsewhere. Even in the modern era, people descend into caves. They use them to hide during wartime, as an alternative to building houses, or to find a cool place away from the scorching desert heat.

On the beach

Coastal caves are created by the sea. The constant pounding of waves throws sand and stones at the cliff face, grinding away at small cracks and making them larger. Eventually the cracks open up into caves. On a headland, this may break right through to create an arch. A large arch may collapse, leaving a single pillar called a stack, sticking up on its own.

THE FRENCH COAST AT ÉTRETAT IS FAMOUS FOR ITS ARCHES AND WHITE CHALK CLIFFS.

FACT 69

AFRICA IS GOING TO RIP IN TWO

The movement of the Earth's plates has created an enormous rift valley across part of Africa, known as the East African Rift. The crust is being stretched, and the eastern part of Africa will eventually split away from the rest of the continent.

On the move

Our continents haven't always looked the way they do today. Around 225 million years ago, there was just a single large landmass known as Pangaea. This "supercontinent" gradually broke apart into separate continents. The theory of continental drift was first put forward by a German named Alfred Wegener (1880–1930) in the early 20th century. He proposed that the existence of mountain ranges at the edge of plates suggested that the plates were moving and colliding.

NORTH AMERICA AND EUROPE ARE MOVING APART AT ABOUT 2.5 CM (1 IN) PER YEAR.

Dino clues

Wegener offered other evidence to support his theory. He noted how the shape of South America and Africa fitted together like jigsaw pieces. He also pointed out that similar fossils are found across the continents, even though they are now so far apart. During the Triassic period, for example, an ancestor of Spinosaurus lived on the supercontinent, and left fossil evidence in both Africa and South America.

Extra evidence

One thing Wegener could not explain was how the plates moved. It took many more years, and several geologists, to do this. Mapping the ocean floor with radar technology, they discovered mid-ocean ridges and seafloor spreading, which gave scientists the evidence they needed to propose that the plates moved around on a layer of semi-molten rock beneath the crust.

Joined apart

Geographers divide the world's landmasses into seven continents, but they are not all clearly separated. North and South America are joined together and are often termed the New World by biologists when giving labels to species. Europe and Asia are a single enormous landmass, but culturally are quite different. Geographers usually include nearby islands as part of a continent, such as Japan which is in Asia.

THE PYGMY MARMOSET IS A NEW WORLD MONKEY, ORIGINATING FROM THE AMERICAS.

BANGKOK IS HOTTER THAN THE SAHARA

Bangkok in Thailand is officially the world's year-round hottest city, with temperatures regularly above 40°C (104°F). They stay this high even in the nighttime, and the humidity is also high, making life here hot and sticky.

FACT 71

The two wettest towns are both in India, and receive around 11 m (36 ft) of rain per year.

Hot spots

It can be hard to know which are the hottest places on Earth. Most of them are so inhospitable that there is no need to set up recording equipment. However, NASA satellites can be used to check surface temperatures. The highest confirmed reading came from the Lut Desert in Iran, at 70.7 °C (159.3°F). Australia's Badlands are close behind, at 69.2 (156.7°F), but many African locations, including the Sahara Desert, regularly reach over 40°C (104°F) in the daytime.

AUSTRALIA IS OFFICIALLY THE DRIEST INHABITED CONTINENT ON THE PLANET.

No sweat

Many of the world's hottest places are also dry. Bangkok is different because of its humidity (the amount of moisture being held in the air). If there is a lot of water, then humidity is high, and it is hard for our bodies to lose heat by sweating. Lower humidity helps sweat to evaporate, keeping us cooler even in high temperatures.

FACT 72

Smells are more easily detected in a humid environment; that's why some humid cities smell pretty bad.

The desert city of Las Vegas is one of the least humid cities in the US.

Damp and dry

Humidity is not the same as rainfall. Although moisture can condense into clouds and fall as rain, that isn't always the case. Arica in Chile is comparatively humid, but still receives less than 1 cm (0.39 in) of rain per year. Measured by rainfall, it is the world's driest inhabited place.

THE RUSSIAN CITY OF VERKHOYANSK HAS THE GREATEST TEMPERATURE RANGE ON EARTH: FROM −67°C (−89°F) IN WINTER TO +37°C (99°F) IN SUMMER.

Sub zero

While high temperatures are rarely recorded by human observers, cold ones are much better known. Antarctica has no towns or cities, but does have research stations where temperatures as low as −89.2°C (−128.6°F) have been noted. At the opposite end of the globe, places in the Arctic Circle also see the thermometer drop to −68°C (−90°F), with Russia staking claim to the coldest towns in the world.

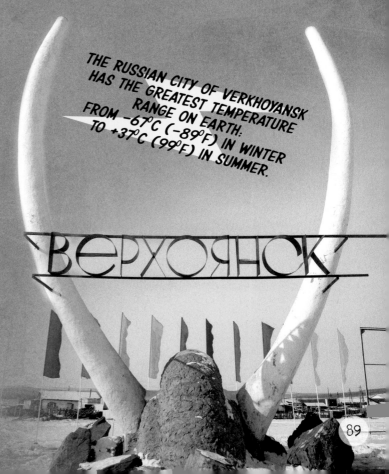

FACT 73 ANTARCTICA IS A DESERT

So little rain or snow falls in the Antarctic that it is classed as a desert. It is cold and windy and most of its water is locked in ice. In fact, it contains 90 percent of all the ice on the planet.

Continent or not?

Antarctica is the southernmost continent, sitting in the Antarctic Circle. It is a solid landmass that is almost entirely covered by an ice shelf. By contrast, there is no Arctic "continent" but an ocean containing many floating ice caps and various islands belonging to different nations. Both are alarmingly cold, but Antarctica easily takes the trophy for the coldest and driest place on Earth. Its average temperature is –55°C (–67°F).

ANTARCTICA IS THE FIFTH LARGEST CONTINENT, BIGGER THAN EUROPE OR AUSTRALIA.

Cold here, isn't it?

At least it's not raining.

Hostile land

The continent nearly doubles in size in winter when the coastal waters freeze. Marine birds and mammals such as penguins, seals, and whales make their home in its icy waters, but no vertebrates live on the continent's interior. There are hardly any plants to sustain life, although certain algae turn the snow pink, red, orange, or green in patches.

Humpback whales feed on krill around the coasts of Antarctica.

Snowstorms

A range of mountains divides Antarctica into two parts, East and West. The ice averages 2 km (1.2 miles) thick on the eastern side but can reach depths of over twice that. The interior is the driest, receiving only 5 cm (2 in) of snow each year. There is slightly more snowfall around the coast. Strong, fast winds sweep up the snow into storms which block out the sky.

Really remote

Antarctica was the last continent to be discovered, in 1820. It took until 1911 for explorers to trek across it to the South Pole. It still has no permanent residents, but scientists visit for weeks or months to carry out research, and thousands of tourists gain special permission to visit on cruise ships each year. They travel across the ice on motor-powered sleds, as no dogs (or any other non-native species) are allowed there.

LESS THAN HALF A PERCENT OF ANTARCTICA'S LAND IS ICE-FREE.

FACT 74
THERE ARE ENORMOUS SAND DUNES IN EUROPE

The Dune of Pilat in France is the tallest sand dune in Europe, reaching nearly 110 m (360 ft) above sea level. Like many sand dunes it is on the move, shifting around 5 m (16 ft) a year as the sand is blown by the wind.

A wealth of choice

As a continent, Europe contains a wide variety of cultures, languages, and even climate types. It is home to the largest country of all, Russia, which takes up 40 percent of Europe's land area. It also has the world's smallest country, the Vatican City, which is only 0.44 sq km (0.2 sq miles), and smallest country with a coastline, Monaco. Despite its small size, Europe is the world's richest continent, with a third of the world's wealth.

EUROPE IS THE SECOND SMALLEST OF THE CONTINENTS BUT HAS THE THIRD LARGEST POPULATION.

A land divided

Geographers have discussed the boundaries between Europe and Asia for centuries, as both sit side by side on one landmass. A commonly used border (dividing line) runs down the Caucasus and Urals mountain ranges. This means that several countries (Georgia, Azerbaijan, Armenia, Turkey, and Russia) sit across two continents. The largest part of Russia is in Asia, but about 77% of the population lives in the European part.

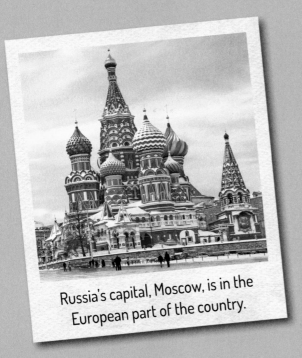

Russia's capital, Moscow, is in the European part of the country.

Happy days

Northern Europe has cold winters with few hours of daylight. Despite that, these countries (Denmark, Norway, Iceland, Finland, and Sweden) score highly in the world's happiness ratings. Southern European countries sit on the Mediterranean and enjoy mild winters and hot summers. A band of Central European countries in between are characterized by picturesque mountain scenery, wide rivers, and large areas of agriculture.

Forest and ocean

After the last Ice Age, most of Europe was covered in forest, and that is reflected in its wildlife even today. Animals such as bears, badgers, foxes, deer, wild boar, squirrels, and lynxes make their home here. The North Sea has around 230 species of fish such as cod, haddock, herring, and mackerel, while the Mediterranean contains over twice that number: about 7 percent of the global total of marine species, including bream, sea bass, sardines, and mullet.

GREECE HAS OVER 200 INHABITED ISLANDS WITH MANY FISHERMEN LIVING THERE.

FACT 75

90% OF ALL RICE IS EATEN IN ASIA

Nearly half of the world's 7 billion population eat rice on a regular basis. Yet, more than 90 percent of the total grown on the planet is consumed in a single continent.

ON MOUNTAINOUS LAND, RICE IS GROWN IN TERRACES. THIS METHOD OF FARMING HELPS TO PREVENT FLOODS AND LANDSLIDES.

Record breakers

Asia is the biggest continent, both in area and the number of inhabitants. Nearly two thirds of the world's people live in Asia even though the continent is only one third of the world's landmass. It contains the world's highest point (Mount Everest) and lowest point (the Dead Sea), and has the longest coastline of any continent. Asia stretches from Turkey in the west to Siberia in the East.

ASIA IS THE ONLY CONTINENT WITH TIGERS LIVING IN THE WILD.

Climate changes

Nearly all of Asia sits in the northern hemisphere. Of course, being so vast, it has many different climate types. Its most northerly areas have extremely cold winters, while countries in the south are hot all year round. Southeast Asia, trapped between the Indian and Pacific oceans, attracts many tourists, drawn to its idyllic beaches, hours of sunshine, and fascinating cultures.

Special residents

Such a huge continent is bound to have a wide variety of creatures. It has its own iconic species such as tigers, Indian elephants, giant pandas, king cobras, orangutans, and Komodo dragons. It is also home to less well-known species such as dugongs, tarsiers, gibbons, Bactrian camels, and slow loris. The distinctive peacock with its splendid tail originally came from India, Pakistan, and Sri Lanka.

Feeling high

China's mountains aren't as tall as others in Asia, but some are equally breathtaking. Candy-striped in a rainbow of red, blue, and yellow, the Danxia range was formed from compressed sandstone over 20 million years ago. Far over on the west of the continent, the Ural Mountains form a natural border with Europe.

DANXIA MEANS "ROSY CLOUD" AND AT SUNRISE AND SUNSET, THE DANXIA MOUNTAINS SEEM TO GLOW.

FACT 76
THE MOON CAN MAKE RAINBOWS

A rainbow is caused by light passing through water droplets. Moonlight can make a rainbow, although moonbows are much rarer and paler than those created by sunlight.

THE BEST MOONBOWS APPEAR WHEN THE MOON IS FULL AND LOW IN THE SKY.

African gems

This moonbow (below) is made by the moonlight passing through spray from the Victoria Falls, on the Zambezi River between Zambia and Zimbabwe in southern Africa. It is one of the places best known for seeing moonbows. The Victoria Falls is classed as the largest waterfall in the world as it is both wide and high, creating an enormous sheet of falling water. Africa is also home to the world's largest desert, the Sahara, and longest river, the Nile.

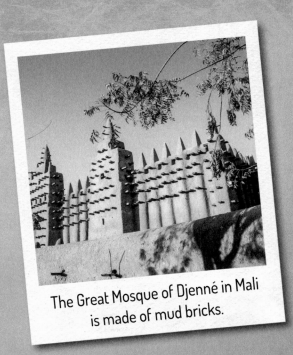

The Great Mosque of Djenné in Mali is made of mud bricks.

A taste of the north

Africa is the second largest continent and is divided in two by the Sahara Desert. Countries to the north are strongly linked to the Mediterranean countries in southern Europe and the Arab states of the Middle East. Their climate suits a wide range of crops such as lemons and oranges, dates, olives, and figs, which are often used in the region's cooking.

Rich and poor

There are riches hidden in the African landscape—literally. More than 40% of the world's gold reserves are here, and 90% of platinum, plus copper, tin, uranium, and emeralds and diamonds. However, Africa is also the poorest continent, with 75% of the world's poorest countries. Approximately 1 in 3 people are undernourished and over 400 million people live in extreme poverty, on less than $1.25 a day.

Southern safaris

Several of the countries south of the Sahara desert are famous for their safaris to see Africa's most sought-after animals. Uganda and Rwanda are home to gorillas and chimps, Namibia and Botswana have cheetah, zebra, leopards, giraffes, and hippos, while Kenya's Masai Mara reserve and South Africa's Kruger Park are noted for the "Big Five"—elephants, rhino, buffalo, leopard, and lion. If it's big cats you're after, try Tanzania. It has more lions than the other safari nations put together!

AN AFRICAN ELEPHANT HAS TWO "FINGERS" ON ITS TRUNK, WHICH CAN BE USED TO PICK UP ITEMS AS SMALL AS A GRAIN OF RICE.

FACT 77 ROCKS CAN MOVE BY THEMSELVES!

Large rocks mysteriously slide along the floor of places such as Death Valley, leaving trails behind them. Scientists only discovered the cause of the motion in 2014, with time-lapse video recordings.

National treasure

Video footage finally solved the mystery of the sailing stones. They are pushed along in ice sheets that break up in the sunshine. So many things about Death Valley are remarkable, from its position as the lowest, hottest, driest place in the US to its salt flats and sand dunes, meteor crater, and mountain peaks with snow on top. Death Valley is the largest national park in the lower 48 states of the US, and some of its rocks are over 1.7 billion years old.

FACT 78 Canada and the USA are the biggest countries in North America, and the second and third biggest in the world.

GEOLOGISTS STUDYING THE MOVING STONES NAMED THEM ALL, WITH THE BIGGEST NAMED KAREN!

Limited languages

North America is the third largest of the continents, and includes the islands of the Caribbean plus Mexico, Guatemala, Belize, Honduras, El Salvador, Nicaragua, Costa Rica, and Panama. North America is unusual since only three main languages dominate: English, Spanish (largely in the south), and French (in Canada and the Caribbean). Mexico has more speakers of Spanish than any other country, including Spain.

The Blue Hole is an underwater cave off the coast of Belize.

Hunting and farming

Much of the land in North America was colonized in the 15th and 16th centuries by European settlers, but native people lived there long before this. Many of them in the north were hunters, while in the south, three great farming civilizations dominated: the Aztecs, Maya, and Inca. They had powerful rulers, complex governments and cultures, and intriguing religions with many gods, temples, pyramids, and even sacrifices.

Land, air, and sea

Every type of habitat can be found across North America, from tundra and coral reefs to deserts and rain forests. Its oceans teem with sharks, whales, and dolphins and its mountains are home to wolves, bears, and cougars. Even its skies are full, and mighty birds of prey such as vultures, eagles, and condors thrive.

FACT 79

Mexico City is the largest city in North America and has a bigger economy than the whole of Peru.

99

THERE'S A TRAIN AT THE END OF THE WORLD

Ushuaia in South America is the southernmost city on Earth, and is often referred to as "El Fin del Mundo" or the End of the World. The steam train there is the farthest south on the planet.

THE SOUTHERN END OF SOUTH AMERICA IS KNOWN AS PATAGONIA AND MANY PEOPLE THERE CAN SPEAK WELSH!

High and dry

Most of South America is in the southern hemisphere. It has the Atlantic Ocean on its east side, and the Pacific Ocean on the other, with the mighty Andes mountain range running down the west coast. In the north, the Amazon river basin, containing the largest rain forest on the planet, covers an area the size of the United States. The continent also boasts the highest waterfall (Angel Falls in Venezuela) and the driest desert (the Atacama in Chile).

Big, big Brazil

South America is the fourth largest continent by size, and fifth largest by population. It has only 12 countries, with Brazil by far the largest. It covers nearly half of the continent! Nearly all the people living in South America speak Spanish or Portuguese, a legacy of the European "conquistadors" who claimed the lands for their mother countries.

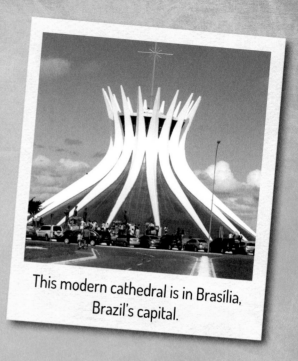

This modern cathedral is in Brasília, Brazil's capital.

In exchange

Many new discoveries were carried back to Europe from South America, including pineapples, potatoes, chili peppers, maize, sunflowers, peanuts, and chocolate. In exchange, the Europeans introduced horses, cattle, sheep, and pigs, farming equipment, and unfortunately, non-native diseases that spread as epidemics because the local people had no immunity against them.

THE AMAZON RIVER USED TO BE A VAST INLAND SEA, AND STILL CONTAINS STINGRAYS.

High altitude animals

The Amazon rain forest has an astonishing array of indigenous creatures (ones that occur naturally in that habitat) but the Andes Mountains also have their own exclusive animals. The vicuña and guanaco are wild relatives of llamas and alpacas and are adapted to life at very high altitudes. The mountains also have one of the highest diversity of amphibians (frogs, toads, and salamanders) in the world.

FACT 81 AUSTRALIA IS WIDER THAN THE MOON

The Moon's diameter is about 3,380 km (2,100 miles), while Australia measures roughly 4,000 km (2,485 miles) across. It is entirely surrounded by ocean, making it the world's largest island. Except... it isn't.

The island continent

Strictly speaking, Australia is an island, but it is so large it is considered to be a continent, not an island. Australia sits on its own tectonic plate and has a very distinct culture and types of plants and animals. It has more than 8,000 islands around it, including New Zealand, New Guinea, and thousands of small Pacific islands. The continent is home to a host of species that are not found anywhere else in the world, particularly marsupials.

FACT 82 People have lived in Australia for around 50,000 years, making their indigenous society the oldest on the planet.

THE PLATYPUS IS FOUND ONLY IN AUSTRALIA, AND HAS A POISONOUS SPIKE ON ITS HIND FOOT.

Seeing red

Most of Australia's inhabitants live around the edge of the continent. Its largest cities are Sydney, Melbourne, and Brisbane in the east, and Perth on the west coast. The huge interior of the landmass has few people living there, and is known as the Outback. Much of it is dry, flat, and rocky, with red-rock monoliths in places, such as the famous Uluru.

Kata Tjuta is a collection of sacred rocks in the Australian Outback.

FACT 83

The world's longest fence runs over 5,500 km (3,400 miles) across southeastern Australia to stop wild dingoes attacking farm animals.

Watch out!

Australia is famous for having many of the world's most dangerous animals. Venomous snakes such as the taipan, death adder, tiger snake, and brown snake live alongside deadly spiders such as the funnel web spider and redback. Crocodiles and sharks also have a fearsome reputation. The oceans are home to lethal stonefish, blue-ringed octopus, and the box jellyfish whose sting can kill a human in minutes.

THE FIRST COMMERCIAL BUNGEE JUMPS TOOK PLACE IN AUCKLAND IN 1986.

Eastern island

New Zealand is around 28 times smaller than Australia but equally fascinating. Its capital, Wellington, is the southernmost capital in the world. Farm animals outnumber people by around 9 to 1, and the country is so narrow that nowhere on the mainland is more than 120 km (75 miles) from the ocean. With many mountains and fjords, it is not surprising that New Zealand is home to the bungee jump. Spectacular glaciers, geysers, volcanoes, forests, and beaches can also be found in the country.

SUNSET IS BEFORE SUNRISE IN ICELAND!

Iceland chooses to be in a different time zone from the one its position on the planet would suggest. That, added to its extremely long summer days, means that the sun sets before it rises!

Clock confusion

Sunset is so late in summer near the Arctic Circle that it slips into the following day. For a couple of weeks in Reykjavik, Iceland, the sun sets after midnight, in the very early hours of the morning. It rises again a few hours later of the same day.

THE TIME WHEN THE SUN IS AT ITS HIGHEST IN THE SKY IS KNOWN AS SOLAR NOON.

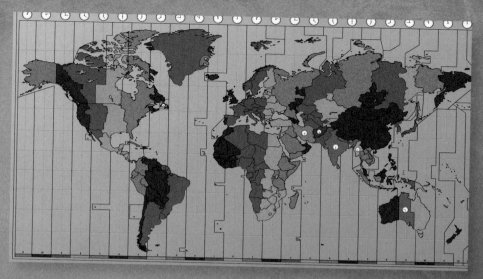

Time zones

Lines of longitude (see page 14) help locate places on Earth's surface. These lines are also used to standardize time. The 0 line passes through London, UK, and places to the east and west of this change time by 1 hour jumps as you move farther away: if it is noon in London, it is 7am in New York. However, these time zones don't always sit comfortably with the Sun's position in the sky. Solar noon can be hours away from noon on the clock!

JAPAN IS FARTHER EAST THAN VLADIVOSTOK IN RUSSIA, BUT ITS TIME IS TWO HOURS BEHIND RUSSIAN TIME.

Drawing a line

Time zones don't follow longitude lines exactly. They zigzag to follow geographical borders. Many west African nations that lie due south of the UK are in the same time zone as London, but Algeria, which sits across the 0 longitude line, stays one hour ahead to avoid confusion within the country.

Lands divided

Very large nations are split into several time zones; the US has six, from Hawaii in the far west across to Florida in the east. However, some countries choose to work to the same time zone across the whole country. Geographically, China should be divided into five time zones, but the government keeps it all on Beijing time. That means that sunset in the far west might occur at midnight.

Washington DC is three hours ahead of the west coast of the US.

FACT 85

BREAD IS MADE WITH FUNGUS!

Yeast is used as a live ingredient in bread to fill dough with gas bubbles and make it rise. Yeast is a type of fungus, a microscopic single-celled organism that divides and multiplies to reproduce.

Simple or complex?

Living things come in many shapes and forms. At their most complex, they are breathing, feeding, moving animals, or respiring, photosynthesizing plants. Simpler organisms are classified into three other kingdoms: fungi, prokaryotes, and protoctists or protists. Scientists differentiate these groups by their appearance and actions but also by the way their cells are designed. They estimate that over 5 million species of fungi exist on Earth.

FUNGUS IS INJECTED INTO CHEESE SUCH AS STILTON OR GORGONZOLA TO MAKE IT TURN BLUE.

FUNGUS CAN BE SEEN ON THE SURFACE OF ROTTEN FOODS BUT HAS ROOT THREADS THAT INVADE MUCH DEEPER.

Breaking down

Fungi cells have a nucleus and membranes. The kingdom includes yeast, mildew, and toadstools and mushrooms. Unlike plants, they cannot make their own food. Instead, they mostly feed on dead plants and animals, breaking them down to help them decompose. The fungi then absorb nutrients through their cell walls. Fungi reproduce by spreading spores through water or the air.

Almost invisible

Bacteria and blue-green algae are examples of prokaryotes. Their cells have no nucleus but do have a membrane, or cell wall. They are often microscopic, but some examples can be seen, such as the green algae coating on the bark of a tree. Although bacteria cannot be spotted with the naked eye, they can be found everywhere, from rocks and soil to your skin and your computer mouse.

Microscopic misfits

Protists are a strange collection of organisms that do not fit into any other category. Their cells also have a nucleus and membranes, but protists are much, much smaller than fungi with only a single cell each. Some can cause deadly diseases. Some resemble animal cells, such as amoeba, which can change shape and move around. They eat by surrounding food with their body.

Most algae are protists and grow in the water.

YOU CAN HEAR BAMBOO GROWING

Bamboo is the fastest growing plant in the world. It can reach 30 m (100 ft) high, and has been recorded as growing over 1.1 m (nearly 4 ft) in a single day. Sometimes it makes a popping sound as the shoots get taller.

Plant life

Plants cannot move to find food, like animals do, but create their own sustenance through a process called photosynthesis. Some rare examples no longer do this, but are parasitic instead and feed on other living things. Generally, plants have roots, leaves, and the stem or trunk. They can be giant trees, or tiny fronds like duckweed. Mosses and ferns are plants, as are all of the fruits, vegetables, and grains that we eat.

MANY BAMBOO SPECIES ONLY FLOWER EVERY 60 TO 120 YEARS.

Liquids of life

The roots of a plant collect water and minerals from the ground. Water helps keep a plant stable and upright; you will see a plant begin to wilt and look droopy if it needs more water. Nutrients and waste are moved around in a watery substance called sap. Some trees produce another liquid, called resin. It acts as protection against injury or insect attack.

The sap of the maple tree can be made into maple syrup.

The sunshine cycle

Plant leaves contain chlorophyll, a green substance which absorbs sunlight. This is used to convert water and carbon dioxide (from the air) into food. Water is drawn up through the stem and reacts with carbon dioxide to make glucose, a kind of sugar. Oxygen is given off during the process, making plants vital to animal life on our planet.

Sweet treat

Glucose is used to make new cell walls, or is converted into starch to store for later. Plants also make fats and proteins so they can grow. Plants are at the bottom of the food web. They are known as producers, since they make their own food. Animals are consumers, which means they cannot make their own food but have to consume plants or other animals.

A TREE'S ROOTS PROVIDE WATER AND KEEP IT ANCHORED IN THE GROUND.

THE DYNAMITE TREE EXPLODES

The sandbox tree which grows in tropical parts of North and South America is nicknamed the dynamite tree since its seeds explode at over 70 m/second (160 mph). They can be launched over 30 m (100 ft) from the tree.

A SUNFLOWER HEAD IS MADE UP OF LOTS OF TINY FLOWERS THAT EACH TURN INTO A SEED.

Spreading the seeds

The sandbox tree uses a novel method of seed dispersal, but the seeds are formed in the same way as all plants. Plants reproduce very differently from animals. They make flowers containing both the female and male parts. The male parts produce pollen, which must be transferred to the female parts of another flower of the same species. When the two meet, they form seeds.

FACT 88

The gas plant produces flammable fumes that can be ignited on a windless day!

Choose me!

Pollination usually happens with the help of the wind or insects and animals. Bees, butterflies, wasps, moths, birds, and even bats land on the plants to feed on the nectar they produce. They brush against the pollen and carry it with them as they visit more flowers. These plants usually have bright flowers with vivid markings to attract lots of pollinators.

Carried on the breeze

Wind-pollinated plants produce lots of light, dry pollen that blows around easily. Many grasses and cereal crops, and trees such as spruces, firs, and pines, are pollinated in this way. Their flowers are often small and dull, with no scent or nectar, since they have no need for showy displays to advertise their wares to passing insects.

Location location

After pollination and fertilization, a flower turns into a fruit. The fruit can be hard, like a nut, or soft, like a tomato or a pear, and contains a seed or seeds inside. The seeds have to be spread far and wide so that new plants can grow away from the parent plant. They can be blasted off, like the sandbox tree, eaten and carried to a new place, or travel by themselves with wings or tiny parachutes.

Some seeds have small hooks so they get carried around on animal fur.

FACT 89 Hayfever is caused by an allergy to wind-dispersed pollen that floats in the air in huge quantities.

FACT 90 SPIDERS HAVE NO EARS!

Unlike people and many animals, spiders don't have ears with eardrums to detect noise vibrations. Instead, they have sensitive hairs on their legs. Many insects also have different ways of picking up sound vibrations.

Hearing aids

Crickets "hear" with their legs, butterflies with their wings, and flies have miniscule eardrum-like structures on their chest. Some hawkmoths can pick up ultrasonic sounds, like those made by bats, with a tiny sensory organ in their mouth. The praying mantis has only a single "ear" by its back legs, and mosquitoes have hearing organs on their antennae. Ants don't have ears either, but detect sounds as vibrations through their feet.

Talk to the legs, man!

BUTTERFLIES, MOTHS, FLIES, AND BEES TASTE WITH THEIR FEET NOT THEIR TONGUE!

Vital invertebrates

Insects and spiders are invertebrates: animals with no backbone. Other invertebrate creatures include crustaceans (crabs, lobsters, shrimps), worms and leeches, jellyfish and anemones, squid and octopus, snails and slugs, and centipedes and millipedes. Over 97 percent of all the creatures on the planet are invertebrates. They are extremely important as they provide food for other creatures, pollinate plants, and dispose of waste.

SCORPIONS ARE ARACHNIDS, WITH EIGHT LEGS, IN THE SAME GROUP AS SPIDERS.

Crazy numbers

The sheer number of invertebrates on the planet is mesmerizing. Compare them to mammals, with around 5,000 species, and birds, with roughly 10,000 species; there are 75,000 species of arachnids, and over a million different types of insect, with more being discovered all the time. Insects are a great source of protein and much easier to farm than cattle, so may become an important food source around the planet.

Growing up

Many insects have interesting life cycles and go through metamorphosis. Their young look very different from their adult form. A fly starts its life as an egg, and changes into a wriggly maggot before reaching its adult form. A moth changes from egg to larva (a caterpillar) and then into a chrysalis before emerging as an adult with wings. A young dragonfly lives as a wingless nymph that looks more like an alien than a dragonfly!

Adult dragonflies only live for a few weeks.

LION CUBS HAVE SPOTS

Adult lions are known for their beautiful golden coat, but their babies have dark spots until they are around three months old. The pattern helps camouflage them in long grass and bushes.

YOUNG LION CUBS ARE PREYED UPON BY LEOPARDS, HYENAS, JACKALS, CROCODILES, AND OTHER LIONS.

Top cat

Even lions need a form of protection when they are young and vulnerable. As they grow older, they become hunters rather than hunted. They are Africa's apex land predator, meaning that they are at the top of the food chain, eating other creatures but not being eaten themselves. Other examples of apex predators are tigers, polar bears, Komodo dragons, alligators, crocodiles, eagles, killer whales, and many sharks.

Chain gangs

A food chain groups together things that live in a single habitat, and places them in the order of what eats what. Food chains usually start with a producer (see page 109), most commonly a plant. Herbivores eat these plants, and carnivores eat the herbivores. A simple example is a rabbit that feeds on grass, and in turn provides food for a fox.

FOOD CHAINS OFTEN END WITH A SCAVENGER OR INSECT THAT EAT THE BODIES OF DEAD PREDATORS.

Tipping the balance

Many food chains can exist in a single habitat, and link together to form a food web. The producer is still at the bottom, but will provide food for several creatures, which in turn are eaten by a variety of others. The balance can be delicate. If the plants are in short supply, because of drought or humans clearing the land, the herbivores may move or starve. This leads to less food for the creatures higher up the web.

Taking in toxins

Other factors can interfere with the food supply. Pesticides, fertilizer, toxic waste, and pollution may enter the food chain at the bottom, and work their way up to the top in larger and larger amounts. Tiny sea creatures called plankton absorb chemicals such as mercury. Small fish eat large amounts of plankton, and become food for bigger game fish such as tuna. When humans eat the contaminated tuna, the mercury levels are higher, and it can make people seriously ill.

Tuna fish are large, fast apex predators.

OVER 430 PARASITES LIVE ON HUMANS

A parasite is a creature that lives on, or inside, another creature. It gets its food from its host (the creature it lives on), sometimes causing harm, but sometimes hardly noticeable at all.

Finding a home

Human parasites include nasties such as head lice, fleas, roundworms and tapeworms, and mosquitoes. They can trigger a rash or itchiness, cause sickness and diarrhea, or lead to deadly diseases. Mostly, a parasite will feed off its host without killing it. Some parasites use their host as transport or as a breeding ground. They can get into the body through contaminated food or water, or from infected animals.

AAARGH!

NITS ARE THE EGGS OF HEAD LICE AND MUST BE REMOVED BEFORE THEY HATCH.

This creepy woodlouse-like parasite feasts on the blood of its host (the fish).

MALARIA, CAUSED BY THE PLASMODIUM PARASITE, HAS KILLED MORE PEOPLE THAN ALL WARS AND NATURAL DISASTERS COMBINED.

Itch-hikers

Humans are not the only hosts for parasites. Many other creatures have smaller creatures living in their fur, on their skin, or in their gut. You can see this for yourself if you have a pet. Pet owners should be particularly careful that their dog or cat does not catch fleas, ticks, or lice, as all of these love to drink blood. Pets should also be treated against worms which can make them and their owners ill.

Living together

Two species that interact closely are said to be symbiotic. Parasites rely on their host for food in a symbiotic relationship that is harmful to one party and beneficial to the other. Cuckoos are an example of a different type of parasitic action. They lay an egg in another bird's nest, and let the mother do the work of hatching and feeding the cuckoo chick.

Here to help?

Some symbiotic relationships can be one-sided, helping one party without harming the other. The barnacles you see on the side of whales do not offer any benefit to the whale, but enjoy a free ride into plankton-rich waters for feeding. Other relationships work both ways. Pollinators (see page 111) get food from flowers, and help the flowers with fertilization in return. Certain birds stay safe and hitch a ride on large herbivores, and eat insects that may bite the animals.

FISH CAN SUFFOCATE IN WATER

Fish breathe oxygen, but they take it from the water rather than from the air. Water is forced out across their gills, and the oxygen dissolved in it can be absorbed into the fish's blood. If too little oxygen is available the fish will suffocate.

Oxygen levels

The amount of oxygen dissolved in water is much lower than that available from the air. Different species need different amounts to breathe: crabs and oysters, for example, that feed on the ocean floor, need less dissolved oxygen than fish swimming in the shallows. The oxygen can enter the water as a by-product from photosynthesis (by seaweed and plankton) or be mixed in by waterfalls and waves.

FAST-MOVING WATER CONTAINS MORE DISSOLVED OXYGEN THAN SLOW OR STILL WATER.

Sailing the seas

Invasive species are a problem in all habitats. Introducing non-native plants and animals disturbs nature's balance and can wipe out established creatures. Large ocean liners have huge ballast tanks to keep them steady in the water. They fill and empty these with ocean water as they travel, carrying new species halfway around the world and spilling them into fresh habitats, causing much concern for oceanographers.

Hotting up

Warm water carries less oxygen than cold water, and scientists are concerned that the average temperature of the oceans is rising. Fish risk suffocating in these warmer areas, unless they swim to other places, damaging the livelihood of local fishermen and disrupting the food chain (see page 115). Shellfish are also affected: increased carbon dioxide in the water prevents them from building their hard, protective shell, leaving them vulnerable to predators.

An algae bloom shows up as green scum on the water.

Plant problems

All sorts of pollution can lower the amount of oxygen available to aquatic creatures. Some rivers are tainted with herbicides (weed killers) that destroy aquatic plant life. The dead plants decay and use up the oxygen in the water, leaving it unfit for fish and other creatures to live there. Other rivers are flooded with fertilizer, causing large algae blooms that deplete oxygen and kill fish.

ELEPHANTS AND HYRAXES ARE RELATED

They may look totally different from each other, but the small, furry hyrax shares its family tree with the enormous, wrinkled elephant. They are also related to the manatee, which spends its whole life in water.

Spot the difference

Scientists find new creatures and plants every year, and try to place them in categories according to their similarities and differences. They also check the characteristics of known creatures to see how they are related to each other, and sometimes revise how they are grouped. Elephants and hyraxes both grow giant incisor teeth to form tusks (in contrast to other animals whose tusks are canine teeth), and females, together with manatees and dugongs, have teats near their armpits. These shared traits link them on the animal family tree.

FACT 95

New species are sometimes discovered in museums! Scientists occasionally realize the specimen they are studying is a totally new species.

What's in a name?

The science of naming and classifying living things is known as taxonomy. One of the most famous taxonomists was Carl Linnaeus (1707–1778) who created a system for naming organisms and arranging them in a logical order, with similar items grouped together. His first categorizations included around 12,000 species of plants and animals. Nowadays, scientists have named roughly 2 million species.

FACT 96

Carl Linnaeus recognized that bats were mammals and not birds, but he classified them as closely related to monkeys!

Dying out

New discoveries are made every year: hundreds, maybe even thousands of creatures that were previously unidentified. However, species go extinct all the time, too. Extinction wipes out all members of a species so that it can never exist again. It happens naturally, but experts are fearful that human exploitation of the planet has speeded up the process by over 1,000 times.

INSECTS MAKE UP AROUND HALF OF THE NEW SPECIES DISCOVERED EACH YEAR.

Splitting up

How are new species discovered? Sometimes, it is simply by looking in new places. Other times, it is by studying the DNA and finding that similar creatures are actually genetically different. This is known as "splitting" and the reverse can also happen. Known as "lumping," some species are linked together when scientists originally thought they were different.

Scientists cannot agree on exactly how many species of lemur there are.

FACT 97 HUMAN BRAINS ARE SHRINKING

For the first 7 million years of human development, the brain grew, almost tripling in size. But for the last ten thousand years it has been getting smaller again. Are we getting more stupid, or don't we need such big brains any more?

FACT 98
The sperm whale has the largest brain of any animal but it is only 0.02% of its body mass.

In proportion

The overall size of an animal's brain is important relative to its body size. Elephants have brains four times bigger than a human, but proportionately smaller when compared to their massive bulk. That helps to explain why elephants aren't smarter than people. Human bodies have become a little smaller as we developed from hunter-gatherers (see page 123) to farmers, but our brains are shrinking at a faster rate.

THE HUMAN BRAIN HAS SHRUNK BY AN AMOUNT EQUIVALENT TO THE SIZE OF A TENNIS BALL!

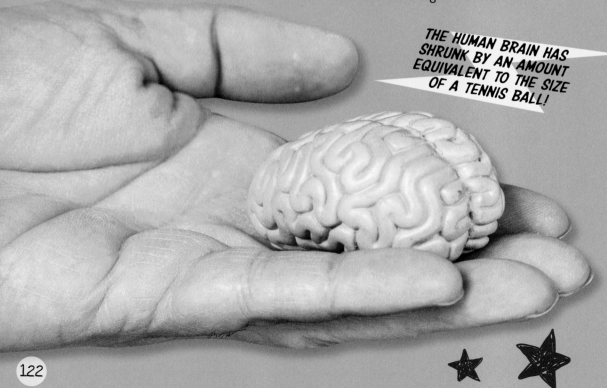

Brain food

Some scientists think the brain has become smaller because of our changing lifestyles. Early humans lived a nomadic hunter-gatherer lifestyle, moving from place to place and eating what they could find or kill. They had to use their brains to stay alive, keeping safe from predators and identifying poisonous food. Gradually, different cultures began to settle in one location and grow their own crops.

The developing world

Towns and cities started to appear, with craftsmen and traders alongside the farmers. People started to own land and build property. Free from the burden of finding food each day, some people became artists, mathematicians, architects, or philosophers. Most early civilizations grew up around fresh water, such as the River Nile in Egypt and the River Euphrates in the Middle East.

Cave paintings show people hunting thousands of years ago.

On the farm

Agriculture developed in many different countries at around the same time. Wild plants were domesticated (chosen for their benefits as food crops) and wild animals were tamed to be useful or kept as livestock. Dogs and sheep were some of the first wild animals to be domesticated by humans, and rabbits one of the last. It wasn't until the Middle Ages, around 1,400 years ago, that people began keeping rabbits for their fur and meat.

FARMING BEGAN OVER 10,000 YEARS AGO AND HAS CHANGED DRASTICALLY SINCE THEN!

FACT **99**

The Aztecs and Incas invented peanut butter!

FACT 100

PARTS OF HONG KONG WERE IN THE OCEAN

Around one quarter of the buildings and roads in Hong Kong are built on land that used to be under water. What was once a small fishing village is now one of the busiest and richest cities in the world.

Room to grow

Much of Hong Kong's territory is mountainous and the land cannot be used for urban development. So the government "reclaimed" land from the ocean, by depositing rocks and mud along the coastline. The same has been done in other countries around the world, making more space for the ever-growing human population. The number of people is increasing so rapidly (by roughly 80 million people per year) that we are filling up every available space.

HONG KONG'S POPULATION IN 1841 WAS 7,450. TODAY IT IS OVER 7 MILLION!

Rising numbers

Before farming, populations were small. The ability to grow food on demand changed that, and population growth accelerated enormously. The number of people on the planet has risen from around five million 10,000 years ago to today's 7.5 billion. People are also living longer, thanks to improved living conditions and medicine. The United Nations estimates that the global total will reach over 11 billion by the year 2100.

Life expectancy around the world has risen by up to 20 years.

AVERAGE LIFE EXPECTANCY IN THE 21ST CENTURY IS 67 YEARS.

People problems

One of the problems with a rising human population is the destruction of Earth's natural habitats. Vast areas of forest are cut down, either to clear space or to use the trees. Industry and farming take over the land and pollute the air and water. Mining and drilling use up natural supplies of chemicals and minerals. All of these leave hordes of plant and animal species without a home.

Running out

People not only need space, they must have resources. As well as food, people need fresh water, energy, and services such as education and healthcare. The more people there are, the more resources are used. Some of them are being used faster than they can be replaced, while others are hard to provide in places hit by drought and disasters. Scientists have to find environmentally friendly solutions to all of these modern problems.

SHARKS ARE EATING THE INTERNET!

Vast lengths of cable stretch underneath the oceans to carry internet signals around the world. Sharks seem to have taken a liking to them, biting their protective casing on the ocean floor!

Shark bait

If the "cloud" of stored electronic information conjures up an image of signals whizzing above your head, then think again. Nearly all of the data that travels around the world does so underwater along over half a million miles of cable. Telecoms and tech companies have invested a fortune in laying them, and now protect them from inquisitive sharks with an extra strong outer layer, similar to a bullet-proof vest.

NEARLY HALF OF THE WORLD'S POPULATION HAS ACCESS TO THE INTERNET, COMPARED TO LESS THAN 1 PERCENT IN 1995.

There are more internet devices on the planet than people.

Time to talk

Communication has changed so much through human history. Spoken language marks people as different from all other creatures, and allows us to pass on knowledge, stories, and customs. This was done on a small, local scale until the invention of printed books in 1440. Since then, radio, television, and the internet have opened up instant communications between all four corners of the world, informing people about things from far beyond the places they have visited.

Let's explore

The great Age of Discovery in the 15th and 16th centuries was a turning point in the way people saw the world. Navigators set sail to find new ocean routes around the globe, and in the process found lands they never knew about. Those who were fortunate enough to return brought with them foreign foods, and specimens of exotic plants and animals.

Distant shores

Today, fast, affordable long-distance travel has shrunk the world and made it much easier to expand our horizons. Scientists can reach far-flung places to study different habitats. Satellites sitting high in the atmosphere beam pictures into our homes, drones can be sent into inhospitable territory, and geobrowsers show us images of unfamiliar lands without us moving from a desk. The modern, technological world seems a much smaller place.

Index